OCCASIONAL PAPER 177

G000055764

Perspectives on Regional Unemployment in Europe

By Paolo Mauro, Eswar Prasad, and Antonio Spilimbergo

INTERNATIONAL MONETARY FUND
Washington DC
1999

Production: IMF Graphics Section
Typesetting: Choon Lee and John Federici
Figures: Sanaa Elaroussi and Theodore F. Peters, Jr.

Library of Congress Cataloging-in-Publication Data

Mauro, Paolo.
    Perspectives on regional unemployment in Europe / by Paolo Mauro,
Eswar Prasad, and Antonio Spilimbergo.
       p.   cm. — (Occasional paper ; 177)
    Includes bibliographical references.
    ISBN 1-55775-800-X
    1. Unemployment—Europe—Regional disparities.   2. Unemployment—
OECD countries—Regional disparities.   I. Prasad, Eswar.
II. Spilimbergo, Antonio. III. Title. IV. Series: Occasional paper (Inter-
national Monetary Fund) ; no. 177.
HD5764.A6M35 1999
331. 13'794—dc21   99-26825
                                               CIP

Price: US$18.00
(US$15.00 to full-time faculty members and
students at universities and colleges)

Please send orders to:
International Monetary Fund, Publication Services
700 19th Street, N.W., Washington, D.C. 20431, U.S.A.
Tel.: (202) 623-7430   Telefax: (202) 623-7201
E-mail: publications@imf.org
Internet: http://www.imf.org

recycled paper

Contents

Tables

Figures

Preface

This paper was prepared by Paolo Mauro, Economist, European I Department, Eswar Prasad, Senior Economist, Research Department, and Antonio Spilimbergo, Economist, Research Department.

Section II draws extensively upon the joint work of Eswar Prasad and Francesca Utili. An earlier version of their paper was presented at the 1998 Villa Mondragone Seminar on International Macroeconomics "Unemployment in Europe Before and After EMU." The discussants, Gilberto Antonelli and Pedro Portugal, provided many useful comments. Section III has benefited from the comments of seminar participants at the International Monetary Fund and the European Economic Association meetings.

The paper has also benefited from discussions with and comments received from Jacques Artus, Leonardo Bartolini, Tamim Bayoumi, Luca Bianchi, Maria Carkovic, Paola Casavola, Jörg Decressin, Enrica Detragiache, Robert Flood, Pietro Garibaldi, Martin Hardy, Alexander Hoffmaister, Yusuke Horiguchi, Andrea Ichino, Pietro Ichino, Alessandro Leipold, Michael Mussa, Alessandro Prati, Danny Quah, Fulvio Rossi, Fabio Scacciavillani, Paolo Sestito, Peter Wickham, and Charles Wyplosz.

The authors wish to acknowledge the research assistance of Madhuri Edwards of the European I Department, and Ivan Guerra and Susanna Mursula of the Research Department. Gail Berre of the External Relations Department edited the paper and coordinated its production.

The opinions expressed in the paper are the sole responsibility of the authors and do not necessarily reflect the views of the Executive Directors, the management, or the staff of the International Monetary Fund.

I Overview

Paolo Mauro, Eswar Prasad, and Antonio Spilimbergo

The third stage of European Economic and Monetary Union (EMU) began on January 1, 1999, with 11 countries having participated in the first phase.[1] To achieve this objective, these countries have strengthened various aspects of their macroeconomic policies, notably their fiscal balances. Some of these countries, however, have had less success in making their labor markets more efficient. EMU will get under way against the specter of persistently high unemployment in many of the participating countries. Reducing unemployment, therefore, remains one of the key objectives across Europe.

While the high aggregate unemployment rate in continental European economies has received considerable attention in the academic literature and in policy circles, an equally important issue is the extent of regional disparities in the employment situation in many of these countries. There are three reasons why large and persistent unemployment differences may be considered a problem. First, they may lead to a higher nationwide nonaccelerating inflation rate of unemployment (NAIRU), with inflation pressures arising in low-unemployment areas sooner in a recovery and spreading to the whole country. Second, they constitute evidence of labor market inefficiency, in that adjustment to past shocks is slow. Third, for a given nationwide unemployment rate, they raise the social costs of unemployment: for example, welfare is lower if one family has two members unemployed and another has two members employed than if each family has only one member unemployed.

Regional unemployment in Europe is thus the focus here. The paper analyzes regional unemployment in a set of OECD countries and finds relatively large and persistent differences in regional unemployment rates in several European countries, including some of the initial entrants into EMU. These differences are indicative of labor market rigidities that raise aggregate unemployment and hinder adjustment to shocks. In particular, wages do not seem to reflect local labor market conditions. As a result, neither capital nor labor migrates sufficiently to reduce regional unemployment differences.

Large and persistent regional differences in unemployment could also have implications for the overall success of EMU, and EMU itself could further heighten regional disparities through three mechanisms. First, since nominal wages will be denominated in a common currency, pressures to equalize wages across EMU countries could intensify, with deleterious effects on aggregate unemployment, as well as regional disparities in countries with relatively low labor productivity. Second, in a regime that is expected to be characterized by low inflation, relative wage adjustment could become more difficult, given that nominal wages are usually not flexible downward. Third, in countries where the exchange rate had mitigated the impact of country-specific shocks that had asymmetric effects across various regions, the loss of the exchange rate instrument could exacerbate the variation in unemployment disparities.[2]

Should EMU result in larger unemployment disparities between regions, the demands for fiscal transfers to high unemployment areas—the tool most commonly used to alleviate the consequences of regional disparities—could breed political and social tensions. Measures to tackle regional differences in unemployment will therefore be needed to avoid such tensions and help in the smooth operation of EMU.

In addition to the cross-country evidence, the paper includes detailed case studies of two euro countries where regional disparities in unemployment are striking—Italy and Spain. Using rich data sets that are specific to each of the countries, the paper correspondingly employs two different sets of empirical techniques that are best suited to each case. The two analyses yield consistent results and are, thus, mutually complementary.

---

[1]These countries were Austria, Belgium, Finland, France, Germany, Ireland, Italy, Luxembourg, Netherlands, Portugal, and Spain.

[2]Such asymmetries are typically due to differences in the composition of output and employment in the various regions of a country.

The section on Italy uses data from different levels of disaggregation to provide a synthetic perspective of the main empirical features of the Italian labor market. In particular, it investigates the possibility that the centralized wage-bargaining system has led to a compressed wage structure within both sectors and regions, resulting in the high dispersion of regional unemployment rates. The findings confirm the widely held view that interregional wage differentials are unresponsive to interregional differences in unemployment and productivity. Using a micro data set that contains information on a large sample of individual workers, more precise measures of interregional wage differentials are computed, controlling for observed worker and job attributes. This micro data set is also used to provide a more detailed examination of the effects of demographic attributes on labor force participation and employment propensities in different regions.

The section on Spain analyzes labor market adjustment mechanisms, using a data set that includes levels of wages, prices, employment, labor force, and output by province. The analysis points to labor market rigidities that increase both regional disparities and nationwide unemployment. In fact, real wages and unit labor costs are found to be similar across provinces, despite large and persistent geographic unemployment differences. The section also estimates the dynamic response of unemployment, participation rates, and migration in the adjustment process to province-specific labor demand shocks.

Both case studies relate the labor market rigidities observed in each country to a number of specific policies and institutional features. Therefore, the results could be useful to policymakers in designing effective policies to improve regional labor market adjustment. In particular, both studies emphasize one important theme: wages are unresponsive to local labor market conditions, which has important consequences for unemployment both at the regional and national levels. The de facto centralized wage-bargaining systems in these countries seem to hinder relative wage adjustment, which would help to reduce unemployment differences. The similarity of unit labor costs, as well as real wages, in low- and high-unemployment areas implies the absence of sufficient "price" incentives for either capital or labor to migrate across regions in response to unemployment differentials, which perpetuates regional disparities.

The paper brings together the policy lessons learned from these diverse empirical approaches. The sections containing the two case studies also present a set of policy recommendations tailored to the circumstances and institutional features of each country. The final section presents a broader set of policy implications.

II Regional Unemployment in Europe

Paolo Mauro, Eswar Prasad, and Antonio Spilimbergo

This section provides an empirical characterization of regional unemployment patterns in European countries. The magnitude of regional unemployment differences is compared across countries and over time. The persistence of these differences is also examined.

Trends in Unemployment Rates

It is useful to begin by examining trends in aggregate unemployment rates. It is well known that the European economies have witnessed rising unemployment over the last two decades, and there is widespread consensus that the structural component of unemployment has also risen considerably. Figure 2.1 plots the average unemployment rate for all EU countries, for the first-stage participants in EMU, and for Italy and Spain.

Nationwide unemployment rates, however, provide an incomplete picture. Trends in unemployment rates have been far from uniform across regions within these countries. For instance, the nationwide unemployment rate has remained relatively flat in Italy over the last three years. This masks considerable variation at the regional levels, with the unemployment rate declining in the northern regions (to its current level of less than 5 percent) and increasing in the southern regions (where it amounts to almost 23 percent).

Perhaps the best measure to summarize the geographic dispersion of unemployment is the standard deviation of regional unemployment rates.[1] Table 2.1 shows the standard deviation of regional unemployment for 14 European countries and the United States. The countries that display the largest variation in regional unemployment rates in 1997 are Italy, Spain, Finland, Germany, and Belgium, in that order.[2]

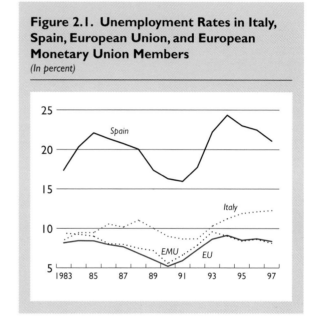

Figure 2.1. Unemployment Rates in Italy, Spain, European Union, and European Monetary Union Members
(In percent)

Most European countries have a greater degree of regional dispersion of unemployment than the United States. Regional unemployment differences increased during the 1990s in several European countries, including Belgium, Finland, Germany, and Italy.[3] On the other hand, these differences declined during the 1990s in Ireland and the United Kingdom.[4]

---

[1]The data used in this section were generously provided by Eurostat.

[2]Caution must be exercised in using the standard deviation of regional unemployment rates for cross-country comparisons because different countries necessarily have different numbers and sizes of regions. This section defines regions as the largest admin-

istrative subunits of a country. The regional disaggregation is based on NUTS-1 (*nomenclature des unités territoriales statistiques*) units except for certain countries for which a finer disaggregation based on NUTS-2 units was required. The definition of regional units is similar to that of Pench, Sestito, and Frontini (1998). For the United States, data on the 50 states were used. The full list of regions is provided in the Appendix.

[3]The unification of East and West Germany in 1990 was obviously an important factor contributing to the increase in both the aggregate level and the regional dispersion of German unemployment.

[4]The Thatcher-era reforms of the 1980s appear to have contributed to the decline in unemployment dispersion in the United Kingdom. For a more detailed analysis of these reforms and their effects on the U.K. labor market, see Prasad and Ramaswamy (1994).

Table 2.1. Standard Deviations of Unemployment Rates

Country	1983	1984	1985	1986	1987	1988	1989	1990	1991	1992	1993	1994	1995	1996	1997
Austria	...	...	...	...	...	...	...	...	...	...	0.90	0.92	0.97	1.05	1.05
Belgium	2.34	2.29	2.52	2.91	3.00	3.14	2.64	2.55	2.42	2.68	3.00	3.27	3.54	3.59	3.59
Denmark	1.97	1.94	1.85	1.38	1.53	1.46	1.63	1.60	2.00	2.15	2.26	2.01	2.04	2.08	1.75
Finland	...	...	...	...	...	3.14	2.50	2.59	3.64	4.80	6.14	6.02	5.39	5.46	5.36
France	1.75	2.14	2.17	2.00	2.07	2.07	2.02	2.02	2.10	2.28	2.12	2.21	2.17	2.54	2.67
Germany	1.71	2.05	2.29	2.25	2.29	2.23	2.13	1.88	2.54	4.03	3.63	3.36	3.10	3.34	4.71
Germany, east	...	...	...	...	...	...	...	...	1.31	1.66	2.46	2.25	2.44	2.16	2.76
Germany, west	1.71	2.05	2.29	2.25	2.29	2.23	2.13	1.88	1.60	1.39	1.61	1.74	1.79	1.89	2.05
Greece	0.98	1.27	2.61	3.71	2.66	1.91	1.75	2.02	1.98	2.49	2.50	2.65	2.66	3.41	2.88
Ireland	0.12	0.40	0.68	0.54	0.58	2.54	1.82	1.63	1.90	1.86	1.81	1.66	1.56	1.40	1.10
Italy	3.10	3.35	3.85	4.87	4.95	6.49	6.60	6.33	5.88	4.79	5.59	6.22	7.00	7.56	7.58
Netherlands	...	...	...	...	...	1.69	1.50	1.73	0.90	1.03	0.97	0.93	0.98	1.33	1.10
Portugal	...	...	...	3.93	3.28	4.24	3.31	2.67	2.28	1.74	1.81	2.41	2.69	2.67	2.29
Spain	3.62	5.20	4.98	4.86	5.28	4.85	5.24	5.46	5.28	5.21	5.49	5.21	5.35	5.52	5.61
Sweden	...	...	...	...	...	...	...	0.68	0.78	1.06	1.34	1.44	1.48	1.43	1.99
United Kingdom	3.45	3.36	3.42	3.45	3.57	3.54	3.68	3.39	2.78	2.42	2.30	2.28	2.23	1.98	2.18
United States	2.53	2.18	1.94	2.23	2.14	1.89	1.33	1.14	1.54	1.61	1.51	1.32	1.28	1.24	1.22

Source: Authors' calculations.

An alternative measure of the degree of cross-regional variation in unemployment rates is the coefficient of variation, that is, the standard deviation of regional unemployment rates divided by the nationwide unemployment rate in each country.[5] This measure, shown in Table 2.2, confirms the high dispersion of regional unemployment in a number of European countries, and notably Italy, Germany, and Belgium, in that order.[6]

Another perspective on regional unemployment comes from examining the dispersion of regional unemployment for different demographic groups. This is of particular relevance in the context of both marked changes in the degree of labor force attachment of some demographic groups, such as females, and considerable increases in youth unemployment.

Table 2.3 shows regional unemployment dispersion measures where the labor force is disaggregated on the basis of age and gender. There are no substantive changes in trends over time or in the ranking among countries in terms of dispersion of regional unemployment when considering different demographic groups. The geographical dispersion of unemployment rates tends to be higher for young workers than for the aggregate labor force. In some countries, such as Italy, youth unemployment rates have been very high in recent years, and the dispersion has been commensurately high.

To show that large regional unemployment differences reflect labor market rigidities instead of large region-specific shocks, the persistence of such differences is analyzed. Specifically, the correlations between the beginning- and end-of-sample unemployment rates for regions within a country are examined.

Figure 2.2 shows scatter plots of regional unemployment rates in 1983–85 and 1995–97 for the United States and for those European countries for which these data are available. Regional unemployment is significantly more persistent in the European countries (with the exception of Denmark) than in the United States. The estimated slope coefficient from a regression of 1995–97 regional unemployment rates on 1983–85 rates is positive for all countries, but the regression's R-squared is markedly higher for most European countries than for the United States.[7] The case of Italy is particularly striking since the correlation coefficient is 0.96.

Why Do Regional Unemployment Differences Matter?

Having examined the evidence on regional unemployment dispersion, it is germane to ask: why regional unemployment differentials matter for overall economic performance; how these differentials can be affected by institutional features and by policy measures; and what, if anything, can and should be done to address these differentials? Moreover, it is important to examine the implications of EMU with respect to these questions.

Regional unemployment differentials could, in principle, result merely from region-specific shocks. Country-specific or industry-specific shocks could also have differential effects across regions, perhaps because of differences in the sectoral composition of output and employment (or in the structure of labor and product markets) among regions.[8] In either case, the dispersion of regional unemployment rates might not appear deleterious per se. However, persistent differentials in regional unemployment rates do suggest inefficiencies in labor market adjustment that could affect nationwide unemployment.

There are also potential feedbacks between regional and nationwide unemployment rates. Layard, Nickell, and Jackman (1991) provide evidence that the relationship between wage growth and unemployment at the regional level is convex in many European countries. Hence, an increase in the regional dispersion of unemployment for a given level of nationwide unemployment would translate into an increase in the nationwide NAIRU. This effect would be strengthened in an economy where a region with relatively low unemployment was the leading region in wage negotiations. This is the case, for instance, in Italy, where wage-bargaining outcomes at the national level have tended to reflect labor market

---

[5]A simple monotonic transformation (the square) of the coefficient of variation is also used by Layard, Nickell, and Jackman (1991).

[6]The standard deviation and the coefficient of variation sometimes reveal different pictures. For instance, in the case of Spain, the standard deviation indicates high unemployment dispersion in absolute terms, while the coefficient of variation indicates moderate dispersion relative to the high level of the nationwide unemployment rate.

[7]Section IV shows that persistence is higher in Spain than in the United States also when using data on the 50 Spanish provinces—the same number of units as that of the United States—rather than the 17 Spanish regions, as in this section.

[8]Bayoumi and Prasad (1997) find that nationwide and industry-specific shocks are more important than region-specific shocks for output fluctuations in the United States compared to Europe. See Clark and Shin (1998) for a comprehensive review of the literature that tries to disentangle these different types of shocks and a summary of the results from different approaches. Since the distinction between region-specific shocks and country-specific shocks that have asymmetric regional effects is not crucial for the purposes of this discussion, they are henceforth lumped together under the rubric of region-specific shocks.

Table 2.2. Coefficients of Variation of Unemployment Rates

Country	1983	1984	1985	1986	1987	1988	1989	1990	1991	1992	1993	1994	1995	1996	1997
Austria	...	...	...	...	...	...	...	...	...	...	0.23	0.23	0.26	0.23	0.24
Belgium	0.20	0.20	0.22	0.26	0.27	0.31	0.36	0.40	0.39	0.40	0.37	0.34	0.37	0.37	0.40
Denmark	0.21	0.22	0.24	0.25	0.27	0.24	0.22	0.21	0.24	0.24	0.21	0.24	0.28	0.29	0.31
Finland	...	...	...	...	...	0.65	0.64	0.67	0.55	0.43	0.37	0.33	0.34	0.38	0.39
France	0.23	0.23	0.22	0.20	0.20	0.22	0.22	0.24	0.24	0.23	0.19	0.18	0.19	0.21	0.22
Germany	0.25	0.29	0.31	0.34	0.36	0.36	0.37	0.38	0.51	0.71	0.52	0.42	0.41	0.41	0.47
Germany, east	...	...	...	...	...	...	...	...	0.13	0.11	0.17	0.15	0.18	0.14	0.15
Germany, west	0.25	0.29	0.31	0.34	0.36	0.36	0.37	0.38	0.39	0.33	0.28	0.25	0.27	0.27	0.26
Greece	0.18	0.22	0.47	0.83	0.58	0.31	0.32	0.38	0.33	0.38	0.36	0.36	0.35	0.40	0.34
Ireland	0.01	0.02	0.04	0.03	0.03	0.16	0.12	0.13	0.13	0.12	0.11	0.11	0.13	0.12	0.11
Italy	0.35	0.35	0.40	0.45	0.49	0.57	0.64	0.68	0.65	0.54	0.54	0.55	0.58	0.61	0.62
Netherlands	...	...	...	...	...	0.17	0.17	0.23	0.15	0.17	0.15	0.13	0.13	0.20	0.21
Portugal	...	...	...	0.47	0.49	0.69	0.66	0.58	0.55	0.45	0.34	0.35	0.37	0.35	0.34
Spain	0.23	0.28	0.24	0.24	0.28	0.26	0.32	0.35	0.35	0.31	0.26	0.23	0.25	0.26	0.26
Sweden	...	...	...	...	...	...	...	0.41	0.27	0.20	0.15	0.15	0.16	0.14	0.18
United Kingdom	0.32	0.31	0.30	0.30	0.33	0.40	0.50	0.49	0.34	0.26	0.23	0.25	0.27	0.28	0.32
United States	0.27	0.30	0.27	0.32	0.34	0.35	0.26	0.21	0.24	0.23	0.24	0.23	0.24	0.24	0.26

Source: Authors' calculations.

Table 2.3. Unemployment Rates on the Basis of Age and Gender
(Average standard deviations)

1983–85

	Austria	Belgium	Denmark	Finland	France	Germany	Greece	Ireland	Italy	Netherlands	Portugal	Spain	Sweden	United Kingdom
Total workers	...	2.39	1.92	...	2.02	2.02	1.62	0.40	3.43	...	...	4.60	...	3.41
Female	...	4.61	2.56	...	3.15	2.37	3.40	1.50	6.08	...	...	5.28	...	2.63
Male	...	1.75	1.76	...	1.59	1.97	1.26	0.35	2.60	...	...	4.77	...	4.04
Workers 24 years old and below	...	4.30	3.19	...	5.95	3.86	3.15	1.57	10.39	...	...	7.18	...	5.95
Workers 25 years old and above	...	2.07	1.59	...	1.32	1.69	1.56	0.43	1.89	...	...	3.59	...	2.58

1995–97

	Austria	Belgium	Denmark	Finland	France	Germany	Greece	Ireland	Italy	Netherlands	Portugal	Spain	Sweden	United Kingdom
Total workers	1.02	3.57	1.95	5.40	2.46	3.72	2.98	1.35	7.38	1.14	2.55	5.49	1.63	2.13
Female	1.41	3.97	1.81	4.90	3.08	4.96	4.88	1.56	9.69	1.39	4.10	6.91	1.04	1.45
Male	0.96	3.53	2.23	5.74	2.26	2.81	2.10	1.80	6.55	0.91	2.04	4.99	2.56	2.71
Workers 24 years old and below	1.81	9.50	2.83	8.51	6.56	2.60	9.10	2.48	18.49	2.38	4.73	7.98	5.07	3.90
Workers 25 years old and above	0.94	3.01	1.81	4.51	2.12	3.99	2.39	1.31	5.56	0.90	2.38	5.06	1.25	1.79

Source: Authors' calculations.

Figure 2.2. Unemployment Rates by Region: 1995–97 vs. 1983–85[1]
(In percent)

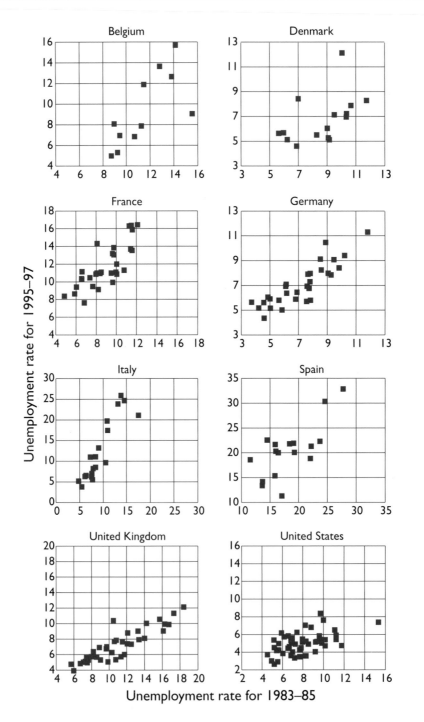

Source: Eurostat, *Regional Statistical Yearbook* (various issues).
   [1]The vertical axis measures the unemployment rate for 1995–97. The horizontal axis measures the unemployment rate for 1983–85.

Table 2.4. Average Net Interregional Migration
(In percent of regional population)[1]

Period	Canada	United States	Germany	Italy	United Kingdom
1970–79	0.62	1.20	0.27	0.37	0.47
1980–89	0.63	0.84	0.34	0.33	0.26
1990–95	0.52	0.87	0.31	0.40	0.20

Source: Obstfeld and Peri (1998).

[1]National figures are population-weighted averages over regions. For the period indicated, each regional figure is calculated as the average absolute value of the change in regional working-age population (measured net of national working-age population growth). The data for Germany refer to the western *Länder* only and exclude Berlin.

conditions in the north, which has had much lower unemployment than the south for many years.

Both capital and labor can play an important role in correcting regional unemployment differences. Capital mobility to relatively high-unemployment areas could take the form of migration of firms, the setting up of new firms, or the expansion of existing firms: new jobs would be created in each of these cases. As for labor, both the migration of labor force participants and changes in the labor force participation rate can help, although these adjustment mechanisms could involve considerable welfare costs. Adjustment through capital rather than labor, therefore, seems to be more desirable and, in particular, the migration of firms appears to be a promising adjustment mechanism. However, given the constraints on data availability, much of the analysis that follows will focus on the role played by prices and quantities related to labor in the adjustment process.

The adjustment to regional employment shocks is an important issue because even temporary region-specific employment shocks can result in long-lasting unemployment if they are not promptly offset by relative wage changes, labor migration, or changes in labor force participation. Given the institutional features and policies in the labor markets of many European countries, temporary shocks could generate hysteresis in regional unemployment rates, which would be reflected in national unemployment rates.

Blanchard and Katz (1992) conclude that in the United States interregional migration of labor is the main shock absorber for regional employment shocks. Using a similar framework, Obstfeld and Peri (1998) compare regional labor market adjustment in Europe to that in the United States and find that regional shocks have more persistent effects on employment in European countries compared to the United States. They also conclude that adjustment through interregional migration is smaller and slower in Europe than in the United States.

Table 2.4 (Obstfeld and Peri, 1998) shows that average net interregional migration is substantially lower in Germany, Italy, and the United Kingdom, compared to Canada and the United States.[9] In fact, as documented by authors such as Faini, Galli, Gennari, and Rossi (1997), labor mobility has been on a marked downward trend over the last two decades in many European countries such as Italy. Since the migration rate may itself reflect high unemployment, it would not be fair to implicate low levels of migration as the reason for inefficient regional labor market adjustment. Nevertheless, an analysis of institutional barriers to migration could have important policy implications.

Some institutional features and policies in European labor markets may well play a role in hindering labor migration. These include transaction costs involved in changing houses and information costs associated with job searches across regions. More important, relative wage rigidities may imply that the "price" incentives to migrate tend to be low. In addition, it has been argued that "cultural attributes" and other intangible barriers limit labor mobility in Europe, both within and across national borders. These influences cannot be denied, although it is not clear why they should play a greater role now than at the time of the massive migration flows of the 1950s and 1960s.

A crucial determinant of the impact of region-specific labor demand shocks is wage flexibility. In fact, relative wage adjustment, rather than employment, could absorb much of the effects of such shocks. However, real wage rigidity is much greater in European countries than in more flexible labor markets such as the United States. Obstfeld and Peri (1998) confirm that relative wage adjustment is

---

[9]In interpreting the data in Table 2.4, it should be kept in mind that migration rates are influenced by the business cycle and that countries could have different cyclical positions during the periods under consideration.

smaller and more sluggish in Europe than in the United States and also in the specific case of the response to regional labor demand shocks. Such relative wage rigidities have adverse consequences at both the national and regional levels.

Wages could also play a useful role in correcting persistent regional unemployment imbalances. If wages were to fall in regions characterized by persistently high unemployment, then lower unit labor costs would attract firms into these regions, and lower real wages would act as an additional incentive for workers to migrate to the relatively low-unemployment regions. In countries that have a centralized bargaining system in which wages are largely determined at the national level, interregional wage differentials tend to be smaller, reducing the incentives for migration of capital or labor.

Regional unemployment imbalances and the effects of region-specific shocks could become more pronounced under EMU for three main reasons: pressures to equalize wages across countries; the implications of lower inflation for relative wage adjustment; and the loss of the exchange rate as a cushion from country-specific shocks for regions that are more vulnerable to them.

First, under EMU, regional unemployment disparities could be exacerbated by pressures to equalize wages across the participating countries. Wage equalization that resulted endogenously from labor migration could, of course, be an efficient outcome. However, it is unlikely that more open borders within the EMU area alone will encourage higher levels of labor mobility across European countries. Thus, the danger is that, since nominal wages contracted in a common currency will be easily comparable across national borders, competition within the EU could result in pressures for wage equalization across EMU. There is also danger in the fact that, with wages but not productivity equalized, unemployment could increase in countries where labor is less productive.

The implications of pressures for wage equalization are highlighted by evidence of significant differentials across European countries in the levels of both labor productivity and labor compensation. Figure 2.3 shows labor productivity levels based on GDP per hour worked and hourly compensation costs in manufacturing in 1997 for a set of European countries.[10] Although international comparisons of wage and productivity levels need to be interpreted with caution, it is clear that there is a substantial dispersion of hourly compensation costs across euro countries, as one would expect in the case of large productivity differentials. If wages in a relatively high-wage country like

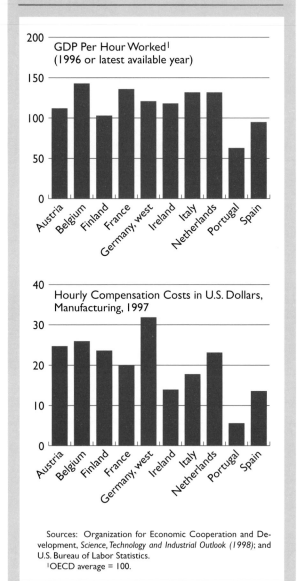

Figure 2.3. Labor Productivity and Compensation

GDP Per Hour Worked[1]
(1996 or latest available year)

Hourly Compensation Costs in U.S. Dollars, Manufacturing, 1997

Sources: Organization for Economic Cooperation and Development, *Science, Technology and Industrial Outlook (1998)*; and U.S. Bureau of Labor Statistics.
[1]OECD average = 100.

Germany were to be used by labor unions in other European countries as the basis for wage negotiations, the resulting differentials between wages and productivity in these countries could have deleterious effects on employment in countries with relatively low levels of productivity, such as Portugal and Spain.

Second, monetary union is widely expected to encourage low inflation, as evidenced by the decline in the inflation risk premium on the government bond yields of EMU countries, including among others, Italy and Spain. Given that the available em-

---

[10]The data on hourly compensation costs in manufacturing are drawn from the U.S. Bureau of Labor Statistics (1997). The data on GDP per hour worked are drawn from the OECD (1998).

pirical evidence supports the hypothesis of downward nominal wage rigidity, the relative wage declines that would be needed in high-unemployment regions could take longer to materialize under EMU than in a context of higher inflation.[11] In the past, the exchange rate may also have cushioned somewhat the asymmetric effects of nationwide shocks in regions with differing sectoral output composition, thereby mitigating in some countries the impact of these effects on regional unemployment dispersion (Eichengreen, 1993), but this will no longer be an option.[12]

Should EMU result in wider unemployment disparities and a more sluggish adjustment to shocks, pressures might intensify for fiscal transfers, which appear to be the preferred tool of policymakers in addressing regional disparities.[13] Such transfers, however, have important adverse consequences. Financing these transfers typically involves distortionary taxation that has a negative effect on overall economic activity. Further, large and continuing interregional transfers tend to breed political and social tensions and often perpetuate the regional disparities that they are intended to cure. Thus, fiscal transfers seem to be a temporary salve, but not a solution to the problem of regional disparities.

---

[11]Akerlof, Dickens, and Perry (1996) provide evidence of downward nominal wage rigidity even in the United States and argue that this phenomenon could have pernicious effects on unemployment in an environment of low inflation.

[12]These considerations are made more relevant by the sluggishness of regional relative price adjustment and the prospect of increased regional specialization under a common currency area. Krugman (1991) notes that regions in the United States are more specialized than European countries, though his analysis is based solely on data for the manufacturing sector. Bayoumi and Prasad (1997) find that, based on a broader one-digit classification of sectoral output, there is less conclusive evidence that U.S. regions are more specialized than European countries.

[13]See Obstfeld and Peri (1998) and the references therein.

Appendix: European Regions and U.S. States

Data from the following European regions and U.S. states were used in compiling the information on regional unemployment rates provided in Section II.

Austria (9)
Burgenland
Kaernten
Niederoesterreich
Oberoesterreich
Salzburg
Steiermark
Tirol
Vorarlberg
Wien

Belgium (11)
Antwerpen
Brabant Wallon
Hainaut
Liège
Limburg (b)
Luxembourg (b)
Namur
Oost-Vlaanderen
Rég,Bruxelles-Cap./Brussels
  Hfdst,gew.
Vlaams Brabant
West-Vlaanderen

Denmark (15)
Aarhus amt
Bornholms amt
Frederiksborg amt

Fyns amt
Koebenhavn og Frederiks Kom.
Koebenhavns amt
Nordjyllands amt
Ribe amt
Ringkoebing amt
Roskilde amt
Soenderjyllands amt
Storstroems amt
Vejle amt
Vestsjaellands amt
Viborg amt

Finland (6)
Ahvenanmaa/Aaland
Etelae-Suomi
Itae-Suomi
Pohjois-Suomi
Uusimaa
Vaeli-Suomi

France (30)
Alsace
Aquitaine
Auvergne
Basse-Normandie
Bourgogne
Bretagne
Centre

Champagne-Ardenne
Corse
Essonne
Franche-Comté
Haute-Normandie
Hauts-de-Seine
Languedoc-Roussillon
Limousin
Lorraine
Midi-Pyrénées
Nord
Paris
Pas-de-Calais
Pays de la Loire
Picardie
Poitou-Charentes
Provence-Alpes-Côte d'Azur
Rhône-Alpes
Seine-et-Marne
Seine-Saint-Denis
Val-de-Marne
Val-d'Oise
Yvelines

E. Germany (8)
Berlin-Ost, Stadt
Brandenburg
Dessau

Halle
Magdeburg
Mecklenburg-Vorpommern
Sachsen
Thueringen

W. Germany (31)
Arnsberg
Berlin-West, Stadt
Braunschweig
Bremen
Darmstadt
Detmold
Duesseldorf
Freiburg
Giessen
Hamburg
Hannover
Karlsruhe
Kassel
Koblenz
Koeln
Lueneburg
Mittelfranken
Muenster
Niederbayern
Oberbayern
Oberfranken
Oberpfalz
Rheinhessen-Pfalz
Saarland
Schleswig-Holstein
Schwaben
Stuttgart
Trier
Tuebingen
Unterfranken
Weser-Ems

Greece (13)
Anatoliki Makedonia, Thraki
Attiki
Dytiki Ellada
Dytiki Makedonia
Ionia Nisia
Ipeiros
Kentriki Makedonia
Kriti
Notio Aigaio
Peloponnisos
Sterea Ellada
Thessalia
Voreio Aigaio

Ireland (9)
Border
Dublin
Ireland

Mideast
Midland
Midwest
Southeast (Irl)
Southwest (Irl)
West

Italy (19)
Abruzzo-Molise
Basilicata
Calabria
Campania
Emilia-Romagna
Friuli-Venezia Giulia
Lazio
Liguria
Lombardia
Marche
Piemonte
Puglia
Sardegna
Sicilia
Toscana
Trentino-Alto Adige
Umbria
Valle d'Aosta
Veneto

Netherlands (13)
Drenthe
Flevoland
Friesland
Gelderland
Groningen
Limburg (Nl)
Nederland
Noord-Brabant
Noord-Holland
Overijssel
Utrecht
Zeeland
Zuid-Holland

Portugal (7)
Açores
Alentejo
Algarve
Centro (P)
Lisboa e Vale do Tejo
Madeira
Norte

Spain (17)
Andalucia
Aragón
Asturias
Baleares
Canarias
Cantabria

Castilla-la Mancha
Castilla y Léon
Cataluña
Comunidad Valenciana
Extremadura
Galicia
Madrid
Murcia
Navarra
Pais Vasco
Rioja

Sweden (8)
Mellersta Norrland
Norra Mellansverige
Oestra Mellansverige
Oevre Norrland
Smaaland med oearna
Stockholm
Sydsverige
Vaestsverige

United Kingdom (37)
Avon, Gloucs., Wiltshire
Bedfordshire, Hertfordshire
Berks., Bucks., Oxfordshire
Bord.-Centr.-Fife.-Loth.-Tayside
Cambridgeshire
Cheshire
Cleveland, Durham
Clwyd, Dyfed, Gwynedd, Powys
Cornwall, Devon
Cumbria
Derbyshire, Nottinghamshire
Dorset, Somerset
Dumfr., Galloway, Strathclyde
Essex
Grampian
Greater London
Greater Manchester
Gwent, Mid-sw. Glamorgan
Hampshire, Isle of Wight
Hereford and Worcs., Warwicks.
Highlands, Islands
Humberside
Kent
Lancashire
Leics., Northamptonshire
Lincolnshire
Merseyside
Norfolk
Northern Ireland
North Yorkshire
Northumberland, Tyne and Wear
Shropshire, Staffordshire
South Yorkshire
Suffolk
Surrey, East-West Sussex

West Midlands (County)
West Yorkshire

United States (51)
Alabama
Alaska
Arizona
Arkansas
California
Colorado
Connecticut
District of Columbia
Delaware
Florida
Georgia
Hawaii
Idaho
Illinois
Indiana

Iowa
Kansas
Kentucky
Louisiana
Maine
Maryland
Massachusetts
Michigan
Minnesota
Mississippi
Missouri
Montana
Nebraska
Nevada
New Hampshire
New Jersey
New Mexico
New York

North Carolina
North Dakota
Ohio
Oklahoma
Oregon
Pennsylvania
Rhode Island
South Carolina
South Dakota
Tennessee
Texas
Utah
Vermont
Virginia
Washington
West Virginia
Wisconsin
Wyoming

Source: Eurostat, *Regions Nomenclature of Territorial Units for Statistics* (1995).

References

Akerlof, George, William Dickens, and George Perry, 1996, "The Macroeconomics of Low Inflation," *Brookings Papers on Economic Activity*: 1, Brookings Institution, pp. 1–76.

Attanasio, Orazio, and Fiorella Padoa-Schioppa, 1991, "Regional Inequalities, Migration, and Mismatch in Italy, 1960–86," in *Mismatch and Labor Mobility,* ed. by Fiorella Padoa-Schioppa (Cambridge: Cambridge University Press), pp. 237–320.

Bayoumi, Tamim, and Eswar S. Prasad, 1997, "Currency Unions, Economic Fluctuations, and Adjustment: Some New Empirical Evidence," *Staff Papers,* International Monetary Fund, Vol. 44 (March), pp. 36–57.

Bentolila, Samuel, and Juan J. Dolado, 1991, "Mismatch and Internal Migration in Spain 1962–86," in *Mismatch and Labor Mobility,* ed. by Fiorella Padoa-Schioppa (Cambridge: Cambridge University Press), pp. 182–234.

Bertola, Giuseppe, and Andrea Ichino, 1995, "Wage Inequality and Unemployment: United States vs. Europe," *NBER Macroeconomics Annual 1995* (Cambridge: MIT Press), pp. 13–54.

Blanchard, Olivier-Jean, and Lawrence F. Katz, 1992, "Regional Evolutions," *Brookings Papers on Economic Activity*: 1, Brookings Institution, pp. 1–61.

Clark, Todd E., and Kwanho Shin, 1998, "The Sources of Fluctuations Within and Across Countries" (unpublished; Kansas City, Missouri: Federal Reserve Bank of Kansas City).

Eichengreen, Barry, 1993, "European Monetary Unification and Regional Unemployment," in *Labor and an Integrated Europe,* ed. by Lloyd Ulman, Barry Eichengreen, and William Dickens (Washington: Brookings Institution), pp. 188–223.

Eurostat, *Regional Statistical Yearbook* (Luxembourg: Statistical Office of the European Communities), various issues.

Faini, Riccardo, Giampaolo Galli, Pietro Gennari, and Fulvio Rossi, 1997, "An Empirical Puzzle: Falling Migration and Growing Unemployment Differentials Among Italian Regions," *European Economic Review,* Vol. 41, pp. 571–79.

Krugman, Paul R., 1991, *Geography and Trade* (Louvain, Belgium: Louvain University Press).

Layard, Richard, Stephen Nickell, and Richard Jackman, 1991, *Unemployment: Macroeconomic Performance and the Labor Market* (Oxford: Oxford University Press).

Obstfeld, Maurice, and Giovanni Peri, 1998, "Regional Non-Adjustment and Fiscal Policy," *Economic Policy: A European Forum* (April), pp. 205–47.

Organization for Economic Cooperation and Development, 1998, *Science, Technology and Industry Outlook* (Paris: OECD).

Oswald, Andrew, 1998, "A Conjecture on the Explanation for High Unemployment in the Industrialized Nations," Economic Research Papers No. 475 (University of Warwick).

Pench, Lucio R., Paolo Sestito, and Elisabetta Frontini, 1998, "Within Countries Unemployment Dispersion in the EU Bloc: Some Lessons for the Forthcoming EMU" (unpublished; Brussels: European Commission).

Prasad, Eswar S., and Ramana Ramaswamy, 1994, "Shocks and Structural Breaks: Labor Market Reforms in the United Kingdom," IMF Working Paper 94/152 (Washington: International Monetary Fund).

U.S. Bureau of Labor Statistics, 1997, *Foreign Labor Statistics* (Washington: U.S. Bureau of Labor Statistics). Available via the Internet: http://www.stats.bls.gov.

III Regional Labor Markets in Italy

Eswar Prasad

As Italy prepares for European Economic and Monetary Union, the potential role of domestic short-term stabilization policies in responding to exogenous shocks has declined. This has brought to the forefront of policy discussions those structural features that could influence the ability of the economy to adjust to such shocks. As in other EU countries, the efficient and flexible functioning of the labor market is of particular importance in this regard and could become a crucial determinant of the economy's long-term growth prospects. Addressing regional disparities in economic performance, which have significant economic and political costs, also remains a key objective.

This section provides an empirical characterization of disparities across Italian regions in the performance of the labor market. The analysis employs a variety of descriptive and econometric techniques and examines data at different levels of disaggregation. This analysis sets the stage for an evaluation of recent reforms aimed at improving the functioning of the labor market and points to directions for further changes.

During the most recent cyclical recovery, total employment has remained stagnant, and the unemployment rate has not declined despite modest output growth. These aggregate figures, however, conceal striking disparities in labor market outcomes across regions. For instance, by the end of 1997 the unemployment rate in the northern part of Italy had declined to about 6 percent, while the unemployment rate in the south was about 23 percent and rising. In addition, there are considerable disparities in employment and unemployment rates across different demographic groups.

This section highlights certain institutional features that have hindered the efficient functioning of the labor market and perpetuated regional disparities. In particular, the wage indexation and wage-bargaining structures prevailing through most of the period examined here have resulted in marked rigidities that have constrained the ability of the economy to respond to adverse macroeconomic shocks. Furthermore, they have resulted in narrow wage differentials across regions, sectors, and occupational classifications that possibly hinder the effi-cient allocation of labor, for instance, by reducing the incentives for interregional and intersectoral mobility. A number of changes and reforms to these institutional features of the labor market have been introduced in recent years.

An evaluation of these reforms and suggestions for further changes based on an analysis of aggregate data are, however, complicated by the fact that such data could mask substantial compositional effects due to heterogeneity in the labor force. For instance, observed wage differentials between two sectors could reflect differences in the average level of human capital in those sectors rather than actual differences in the underlying wage distributions. Data from the 1995 household survey conducted by the Bank of Italy are used to control for such observable worker characteristics and to gain a more precise understanding of the wage structure. This micro data set is also used to examine the determinants of employment and labor force participation propensities. This analysis, combined with direct evidence from the survey on the characteristics of unemployed workers and reasons for non-participation in the labor force, provides insights that could be useful for designing measures to improve the efficient functioning of labor markets.

Main Empirical Features

This section first reviews the main empirical features of the Italian labor market from an aggregate perspective. An examination of disaggregated data is then used to show that the aggregate data mask substantial variations in labor market developments across different regions and across demographic groups. These differences could have important implications for formulating and implementing labor market policy.

As in other European countries, the unemployment rate in Italy has drifted upward over the last two decades (Figure 3.1, upper panel). The aggregate unemployment rate, however, masks enormous differences in regional unemployment rates. The differential between the unemployment rates in the south and the north has widened markedly since the

Figure 3.1. Unemployment and Employment Growth
(In percent)

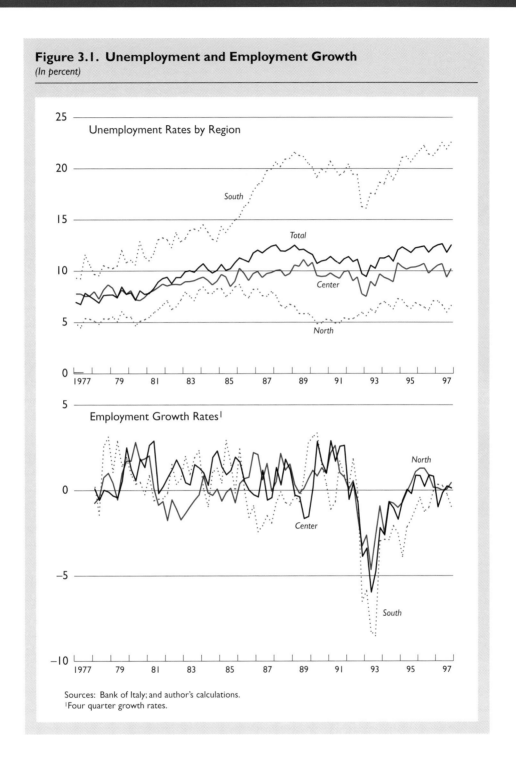

Sources: Bank of Italy; and author's calculations.
[1]Four quarter growth rates.

1970s. By the end of 1997, the unemployment rate was about 6 percent in the north, 10 percent in the center, and 23 percent in the south.

A notable feature of the recent recovery has been the widening differential between unemployment rates in the north and south. While the unemployment rate in the north has declined during the recov-ery, it has continued to increase in the south, reaching a historical high in 1997.[1] Figure 3.1 (lower

---

[1]See Pugliese (1993) for additional perspectives on the regional segmentation of the Italian labor market relative to other European labor markets.

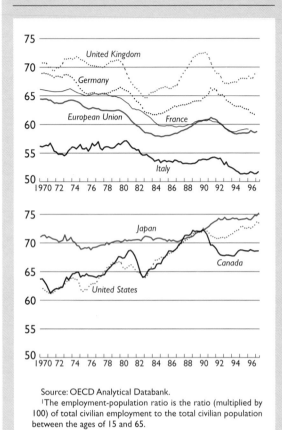

Figure 3.2. Employment-Population Ratios[1]: A Cross-Country Perspective
(In percent)

Source: OECD Analytical Databank.
[1]The employment-population ratio is the ratio (multiplied by 100) of total civilian employment to the total civilian population between the ages of 15 and 65.

The unemployment rate is affected not just by developments in employment but also by changes in labor force participation rates that could be related to the business cycle as well as to longer-term factors. To abstract from the effects of such changes and to obtain a more accurate picture of the evolution of employment and nonemployment, it is useful to examine the employment-population ratio, defined as the ratio of employed persons to all potential labor force participants between the ages of 15 and 65.[2]

Figure 3.2 shows the employment-population ratio in Italy and also provides a cross-country comparison. This ratio has declined gradually in Italy since the early 1980s; in 1997, it stood at 52 percent. A striking fact is that, historically, this ratio has been much lower in Italy than in most other continental European countries and substantially lower than the ratios in Japan and the Anglo-Saxon countries. These figures imply that, even at those times during the last three decades when the Italian economy could be characterized as being at "full employment," the employment-population ratio was under 60 percent—well below the corresponding ratios for other countries shown here. These data indicate a higher rate of nonemployment among potential labor force participants in Italy than in other countries. This low employment-population ratio, based on official employment statistics, could reflect in part the higher share of employment in the informal sector in Italy than in other industrialized economies.[3]

The relatively stable aggregate employment-population ratio, however, conceals large disparities in the level and evolution of this ratio for males and females. Figure 3.3 (upper panel) shows that the employment-population ratio for males has declined gradually to about 72 percent in 1997 from 85 percent in the mid-1970s. The employment-population ratio for females rose to about 40 percent in 1990 from 35 percent in the mid-1970s and has since remained essentially unchanged. Figure 3.3 (lower panel) also shows that the labor force participation rate for males has declined by about 10 percentage points over the last two decades, offset by a corresponding increase in the participation rate for females. The increasing presence of women in the labor force and in employment is similar to the experience of other industrialized countries. Nevertheless, the participation and employment rates of women in Italy remain far below those in most other industrialized countries.

panel) shows that, during the recent recession, sustained negative employment growth over a period of three to four years resulted in employment losses that were especially large in the south. Employment in the south has only recently stabilized, after almost four years of successive declines, leaving the level of employment in the region substantially below that prevailing in 1992. Employment growth rates in the north and center, on the other hand, turned positive in the latter half of 1995 but have tapered off since early 1997.

As noted in Section II, the dispersion of regional unemployment rates in Italy is the largest among the OECD countries. Although other EU countries, such as Belgium, Germany, and Spain, also have significant regional disparities in unemployment rates, an important difference is that in all of these countries changes in regional unemployment rates have been positively correlated during the 1990s.

---

[2]These age brackets were chosen to facilitate international comparison. The minimum working age in Italy is 14.

[3]The existence of a large informal sector may in turn be attributable, among other factors, to the fact that Italy has one of the highest tax wedges among the OECD countries.

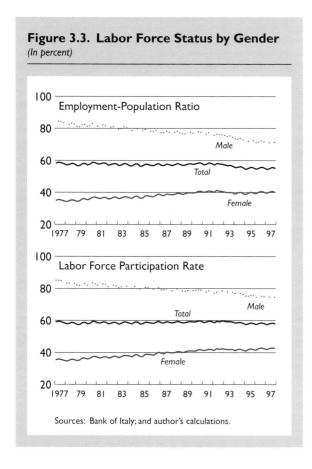

Figure 3.3. Labor Force Status by Gender
(In percent)

Employment-Population Ratio

Male

Total

Female

1977 79 81 83 85 87 89 91 93 95 97

Labor Force Participation Rate

Male

Total

Female

1977 79 81 83 85 87 89 91 93 95 97

Sources: Bank of Italy; and author's calculations.

Figure 3.4. Employment and Participation Rates by Region
(In percent)

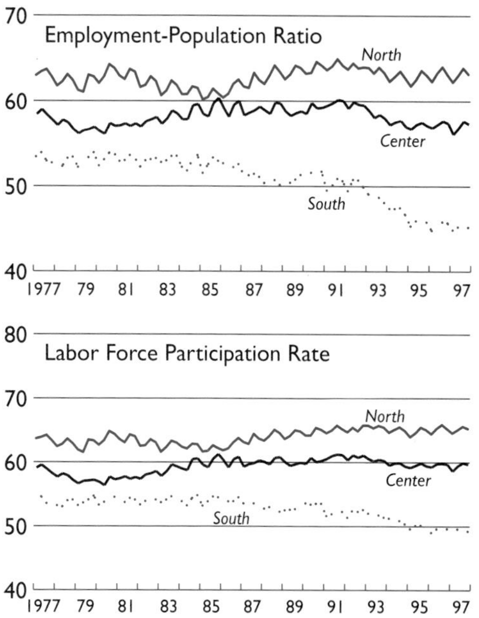

Employment-Population Ratio

North

Center

South

1977 79 81 83 85 87 89 91 93 95 97

Labor Force Participation Rate

North

Center

South

1977 79 81 83 85 87 89 91 93 95 97

Sources: Bank of Italy; and author's calculations.

Figure 3.4 (top panel) shows employment-population ratios broken down by region. Not only has this ratio been lower in the south of Italy, compared to the northern and central regions, but it has declined in the south since 1990 and continued to decline—although at a slower rate—even during the recent recovery. In all three areas, the employment-population ratio for males has fallen over the last decade, but the decline has been especially sharp in the south. The female employment-population ratio has increased gradually since the 1970s in the north and center, but it has remained essentially flat—at a low level of less than 30 percent—in the south.

The lower panel of Figure 3.4, which shows labor force participation rates broken down by region, also indicates marked regional differences: a high and relatively stable participation rate in the north and center, and a low and declining rate in the south. While participation rates for males have fallen over the last two decades in all three areas, the rates for women have increased significantly in the north and center but not in the south.

To summarize, in terms of labor force participation and employment in the formal sector, there is clear evidence of segmentation of the Italian labor market across regions. Compared to other industrial countries, aggregate participation and employment are both relatively low. In particular, constraints on the female labor supply, which until recently included the lack of temporary and flexible work arrangements that tend to induce more women to enter the labor force, appear to be significant in Italy and particularly acute in the south.

Wage Dispersion

An important determinant of the ability of different economic sectors to respond to macroeconomic shocks is the degree of aggregate, as well as disaggregate, wage flexibility. Industry- and region-specific shocks play an important role in economic fluctuations in most industrial countries.[4] Rigidities

---

[4]Bayoumi and Prasad (1997) find that, for Italy, industry-specific shocks are more important than common shocks across all industries for explaining fluctuations in disaggregated output growth.

in wage differentials across sectors and across regions could result in temporary shocks having permanent effects on employment and unemployment. Furthermore, wage differentials that do not accurately reflect productivity differentials are likely to constrain the adjustment of labor markets to exogenous shocks and hinder the efficient allocation of labor by reducing the incentives for labor mobility. This is evidenced, for instance, by the steady decline over the last decade in interregional migration despite the widening disparity of regional unemployment rates.[5]

Certain institutional features appear to have contributed to a suboptimal degree of wage differentiation in Italy. In an attempt to promote greater wage equality, the wage indexation scheme known as the *scala mobile* was modified in 1975 to provide similar cost of living adjustments for all workers, independent of their earning levels. This resulted in a sharp compression of wage differentials across occupational classifications in the 1970s. The 1983 reform of the indexation system halted the decline in wage differentiation, and the indexation system was abolished altogether in 1992.[6]

The centralized wage-bargaining system has also contributed to the relatively small intersectoral and interregional wage differentials in Italy compared to most other industrialized countries. The wage-bargaining procedure resulted in legally binding wage floors that were negotiated for each sector by category of occupation between the unions and employers at a central level and that were then applied uniformly across regions. Since negotiated wage floors have traditionally accounted for a substantial portion of most workers' earnings, this centralized bargaining procedure resulted in relatively narrow wage differentials across regions and also across sectors (possibly reflecting coordination by national unions).

The new wage-negotiating framework, introduced in 1993, formalized a two-level wage-bargaining structure, where the second level of bargaining was not limited to larger firms, as had been the case before. Within this framework, national contracts for each industry determine the structure and evolution of wages over a two-year period and determine employment terms and working conditions over a four-year period. These industry-level wage contracts are established in a manner consistent with official inflation targets. The second level of bargaining is at the individual enterprise level and allows wages to be linked to productivity or profitability indicators.

The change from a relatively centralized to a decentralized wage-bargaining system carries both risks and opportunities. As noted by Calmfors and Driffill (1988) and Calmfors (1993), there is likely to be a nonmonotonic relationship between the degree of centralization of wage bargaining and labor market outcomes. Centralized unions are more likely to internalize the externalities inherent in the fact that they are more beholden to "insiders" than to unemployed workers who are not union members. On the other hand, centralized unions could lead to lower wage differentiation, as has been the case in Italy. Furthermore, these factors interact with the degree of union power and the degree of coordination among unions in the wage-setting process.[7] Hence, it is difficult to determine precisely the optimal wage-bargaining structure for maximizing social welfare.

Nevertheless, given the changes in the wage-bargaining structure and other aspects of wage formation, it is useful to provide a preliminary empirical assessment of the effects of these reforms on wage dispersion. Figure 3.5 shows the dispersion—as measured by the standard deviation—of (the logarithms of) nominal wages for dependent employees in 11 industries using 3 alternative wage series: the minimum contractual hourly wage indices for laborers, the minimum contractual wage per employee for all workers, and the minimum contractual wage per employee for laborers.

The wage indexation system resulted in a significant compression of wage differentials during the 1970s, both across sectors and across skill groups (see Erickson and Ichino, 1995). The sharp decline in the sectoral dispersion of wages during this period is evident for all three measures of wages. Changes to the wage indexation system in the mid-1980s resulted in an increase in wage dispersion but, thereafter, wage differentials across sectors continued to decline gradually. Since 1995, however, the sectoral dispersion of wages appears to have risen, as evidenced by increases in all three dispersion measures. This suggests that the 1992–93 changes in wage-bargaining arrangements have been effective in promoting flexibility in the sectoral wage structure by, inter alia, providing an enhanced role for contracts at

---

[5]Faini, Galli, Gennari, and Rossi (1997) document trends in interregional migration in Italy. Based on survey evidence, they also list a number of institutional factors, such as an inflexible housing market, that have hindered migration within Italy.

[6]The 1983 reform of the indexation system included a 15 percent reduction in inflation coverage. As discussed by Bertola and Ichino (1995b), the indexation system was then progressively weakened. In particular, a cap was instituted on *scala mobile* payments in 1984, and cost of living adjustments were made proportional to earnings in 1986.

[7]Decentralized wage bargaining could enhance wage differentiation but could lead to a wage-price spiral if relative wage competition among unions is significant, thereby resulting in adverse effects on aggregate employment.

Figure 3.5. Measures of Interindustry Wage Dispersion

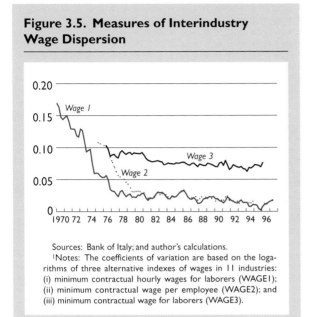

Sources: Bank of Italy; and author's calculations.
[1]Notes: The coefficients of variation are based on the logarithms of three alternative indexes of wages in 11 industries: (i) minimum contractual hourly wages for laborers (WAGE1); (ii) minimum contractual wage per employee (WAGE2); and (iii) minimum contractual wage for laborers (WAGE3).

the enterprise level that explicitly link wage settlements to measures of productivity and profitability. The substantial compression of sectoral wage differentials relative to historical levels suggests, however, that the Italian labor market remains relatively inflexible in this dimension and that further progress is necessary.[8]

A similar examination of regional wage differentials is hampered by a lack of reliable wage data disaggregated at the regional level. Furthermore, differences in industrial structures across regions could influence observed interregional wage differentials. To overcome these problems and to provide a finer characterization of employment and wage structures, a more detailed analysis using micro data is required.

The Structure of Earnings and Employment: Evidence from Micro Data

This section presents an alternative perspective on the regional segmentation of the Italian labor market. Individual data from the Bank of Italy's house-

hold survey are used to analyze the wage structure in more detail. Furthermore, evidence from this microdata set on the reasons for unemployment and for nonparticipation in the labor force could help gain some insights into factors that affect employability and labor supply decisions.

Earnings

Average measures of wage differentials across regions and across sectors may be contaminated by aggregation bias due to worker heterogeneity. For instance, an apparently large average wage differential between two sectors could simply reflect differences in the average level of human capital of workers in the two sectors. Micro (individual) data may be used to control for observed worker attributes and thereby provide more accurate measures of wage differentials. In addition, such data may also be used to obtain measures of wage differentials between male and female workers, across different skill levels, across different firm sizes, etc., that control for other observed attributes of workers.[9]

The data used in this part of the analysis are drawn from the 1995 version of the Bank of Italy's household survey, which includes data on individual workers' earnings and other characteristics. Summary statistics for the data samples are presented in Table 3.1.[10] The analysis of the wage structure is limited here to dependent workers (employees) and excludes self-employed workers. An important caveat is that the earnings data represent net earnings. Given the progressivity of the income tax structure, this could, in principle, understate wage differentials across, for instance, skilled (high-wage) and unskilled (low-wage) workers. Since the tax structure is similar across regions and local income taxes are not significant, estimates of regional wage differentials are less likely to be affected by this feature of the data.

---

[8]The OECD estimates that the coefficient of variation of labor cost levels per working hour for production workers across 13 industries in the manufacturing sector was 0.15 in Italy in 1994—compared to about 0.30 for Canada, Japan, and the United States—and an average of 0.20 for France, Germany, Spain, and the United Kingdom (OECD, 1997).

[9]See Keane and Prasad (1996) for a discussion and an empirical example of how estimates of sectoral wage equations using data aggregated at an economywide or sectoral level can be biased by compositional effects.

[10]The survey is based on a stratified sample where the basic sampling unit is the household. Over- or undersampling of particular groups and differences in nonresponse rates across sub-strata imply that the sample may not be fully representative. Sampling weights that can be used to correct for this lack of representativeness are provided by the Bank of Italy but, because individual rather than household data are used here, these weights are not necessarily appropriate for the purposes of this paper. Nevertheless, when the regressions reported in this section were run using these sampling weights, the estimated coefficients differed only marginally from those reported in the paper. Results from the weighted regressions are available from the author.

Table 3.1. Summary Statistics for Data Samples
(Sample means)

	Wage Regressions	Employment Equations	Labor Force Participation Equations
North	0.48	0.43	0.41
Center	0.21	0.21	0.21
South	0.31	0.37	0.38
Less than high school diploma	0.46	0.50	0.59
High school diploma	0.42	0.39	0.34
College degree	0.12	0.11	0.07
Male	0.61	0.62	0.50
Married workers	0.66	0.61	0.59
Married female workers	—	0.21	0.31
Urban	0.94	0.93	0.93
Experience (in years)	24.64	23.81	24.19
Invalid	0.02	0.03	0.03
Sick	0.11	0.11	0.14
Employed	—	0.83	—
Number of observations	6,222	9,971	16,971

Sources: Bank of Italy, *Household Survey* (1995); and author's calculations.

Notes: All variables shown above, except experience, are dummy variables. This implies, for instance, that 48 percent of the observations used in the wage regressions are for workers who live in the north.

Empirical analysis of the wage structure is based on ordinary least squares regressions of the form:

$$\log e_i = \alpha + \beta X_i + \sum_{j=1}^{k} \gamma_j I_{ij} + \in_i, \qquad (3.1)$$

where e_i represents average weekly earnings of worker i and X_i is a vector of individual-specific characteristics that also includes job-specific variables, such as the size of the firm that employs the worker. I_j is an indicator of the sector of occupation; this set of indicator variables is omitted in the sectoral regressions.

Table 3.2 provides results for regressions of weekly earnings. The first column of the table shows the results from the regression using the full sample of employed workers. The estimated coefficients on the industry dummies are shown in one of the bottom rows of the table (relative premium). These coefficients represent estimates of earnings differentials across sectors relative to earnings in the manufacturing sector. Since the earnings variable is expressed in logarithms, the coefficient estimates are interpretable as percentage differences relative to average earnings in manufacturing.

Average earnings in agriculture are estimated to be about 60 percent lower than in manufacturing. Among other sectors, however, the earnings differentials are generally quite narrow. There is a negligi-

ble differential between earnings in manufacturing and average earnings in trade, transport and communications, and real estate. As in other countries, earnings in the household and personal services sector are lower than in manufacturing, while earnings in the financial sector are among the highest.

The coefficients on the dummy variables center and south (in the first column) capture the estimated earnings differentials of workers in these regions relative to workers in the north, after controlling for worker characteristics as well as sector of occupation. These coefficient estimates indicate that, relative to the north, average earnings are 8 percent lower in the center and 18 percent lower in the south.

The earnings premium for workers with a high school diploma compared to those who do not have a high school diploma is 19 percent. Workers with a college degree earn an additional premium of about 10 percent. The large earnings premium for workers with higher levels of general human capital is consistent with other evidence of large and increasing skill premia resulting from skill-biased technological change since the 1970s and is similar to evidence that has been documented for other industrial countries. The coefficient on the dummy variable for males indicates that male workers on average have 28 percent higher earnings than female workers,

Table 3.2. Wage Regressions for Logarithms of Net Weekly Earnings

	All	Agriculture	Manufacturing	Construction	Trade	Transport and Communications	Finance	Real Estate	Household and Personal Services	Government
Center	-0.08* (0.02)	0.28 (0.20)	-0.07* (0.03)	-0.18 (0.09)	-0.17* (0.06)	0.08 (0.10)	-0.02 (0.07)	-0.20 (0.10)	-0.19* (0.08)	-0.04 (0.02)
South	-0.18* (0.02)	-0.49* (0.15)	-0.16* (0.03)	-0.40* (0.07)	-0.28* (0.05)	-0.15 (0.09)	-0.11 (0.07)	-0.28* (0.10)	-0.25* (0.08)	-0.09* (0.02)
High school diploma	0.19* (0.01)	0.46* (0.16)	0.18* (0.02)	0.30* (0.08)	0.10* (0.05)	0.23* (0.08)	0.11 (0.10)	0.00 (0.11)	0.17* (0.08)	0.17* (0.02)
College degree	0.30* (0.02)	-0.52 (0.59)	0.43* (0.06)	0.22 (0.27)	0.52* (0.14)	0.25 (0.17)	0.46* (0.11)	-0.05 (0.16)	-0.15 (0.22)	0.23* (0.03)
Male	0.28* (0.01)	0.54* (0.12)	0.26* (0.02)	0.21 (0.14)	0.28* (0.04)	0.51* (0.11)	0.17* (0.07)	0.24* (0.09)	0.54* (0.07)	0.23* (0.02)
Firm size (ii) (20–99)	0.16* (0.02)	0.12 (0.16)	0.12* (0.03)	0.23* (0.07)	0.15* (0.06)	0.03 (0.12)	0.25* (0.11)	0.26* (0.11)	0.28* (0.09)	...
Firm size (iii) (100–499)	0.24* (0.03)	0.54* (0.22)	0.20* (0.03)	0.30* (0.13)	0.19* (0.10)	-0.21 (0.12)	0.46* (0.09)	0.47* (0.18)	0.23* (0.11)	...
Firm size (iv) (over 500)	0.30* (0.02)	0.29 (0.59)	0.30* (0.03)	0.28* (0.14)	0.15* (0.08)	0.31* (0.10)	0.32* (0.07)	0.41* (0.16)	0.28* (0.13)	...
Relative premium	...	-0.60* (0.04)	...	-0.16* (0.03)	-0.03 (0.02)	0.06 (0.04)	0.28* (0.04)	0.00 (0.04)	-0.24* (0.03)	0.22* -0.02
Adjusted R squared	0.38	0.31	0.34	0.23	0.26	0.39	0.50	0.37	0.28	0.23
Number of observations	6,222	180	1,851	351	670	190	225	179	300	2,276

Sources: Bank of Italy, *Household Survey* (1995); and author's calculations.

Notes: The firm size dummy variables are based on the total number of registered employees (indicated in parentheses) in the establishment. The relative premium is the estimated average sectoral earnings premium relative to the manufacturing sector, expressed as a percentage of average earnings in manufacturing. These premiums were computed from the coefficients on the industry dummies in the regression with "all" observations (column I). The additional controls included in the regressions are experience and its square, and the following dummy variables: married, urban, invalid, and sick (persons with chronic diseases). An asterisk indicates statistical significance at the 5 percent level.

even after controlling for education levels, labor market experience, region and sector of employment, and other observable attributes. The coefficient estimates for the firm size dummies clearly show that, even after controlling for observed worker characteristics, workers in larger firms have significantly higher earnings.[11]

The estimated sectoral and regional earnings differentials for 1995 suggest that the labor market reforms introduced in 1992–93 do appear to have helped in fostering some degree of wage differentiation.[12] It is useful in this context to examine regional and other aspects of differentials within each sector. Hence, the earnings regressions were also run separately for workers in each sector. The only difference relative to the regression for the full sample is that the sectoral dummies were excluded. The sector-specific wage regressions are reported in columns 2–10 of Table 3.2.

The north-south earnings differentials are greater in industries such as construction and, particularly, in industries that typically have lower union densities—including agriculture, real estate, and household and personal services. Not surprisingly, the regional differentials are among the smallest in public administration. The existence of a statistically and economically significant earnings premium for workers in larger firms is a robust finding across virtually all sectors of the private economy.

A different perspective on the wage structure is provided by using hourly, rather than weekly, earnings. Employment contracts may stipulate specific weekly earnings but, as part of an implicit bargain between firms and employees, both regular and overtime hours could bear the brunt of adjustment in response to changes in demand conditions. Table 3.3 provides results from wage regressions similar to those given in Table 3.2 but using hourly earnings as the dependent variable.

The regression with all observations (column 1) shows that differentials in hourly wages between the north and the south are about 12 percent—much lower than the estimated weekly earnings differential of 18 percent. Thus, measures of weekly earnings appear to overstate the extent of interregional wage differentiation. The estimated premium for

workers with a high school diploma remains about 19 percent, but the hourly earnings premium for workers with a college degree compared to workers with only a high school diploma increases to 28 percent (0.46–0.18)—much larger than the weekly earnings premium. The male-female earnings differential, on the other hand, drops to 9 percent when measured by hourly earnings. The estimated effect of firm size on earnings remains essentially unchanged.

The estimated sectoral differentials for hourly wages, shown in the "relative premium" row of Table 3.3, are in many cases quite different from the differentials in weekly earnings. For instance, the average hourly earnings differential between agriculture and manufacturing is close to zero, compared to the 60 percent differential in weekly earnings. This discrepancy reflects the substantially lower average weekly hours worked in agriculture compared to manufacturing. Another notable feature of these results is the considerably lower dispersion of hourly earnings across sectors compared with the dispersion of weekly earnings.

The results of sectoral wage regressions using the hourly earnings measures are given in columns 2–10 of Table 3.3. Consistent with the aggregate results, these results show that in most industries the north-south differentials in hourly earnings are lower than the differentials in weekly earnings that do not adjust for hours worked. For some sectors, such as transport and communications, financial services, and government, there are essentially no significant differences in wages between the north and the south.

In summary, when using measures of weekly earnings there are some indications of statistically and economically significant earnings differentials among geographical regions and across broad sectors of the economy. However, after adjusting for weekly hours worked, it appears that actual differentials in hourly earnings remain quite narrow.

Employment, Unemployment, and Nonemployment

Data from the household survey can also be used to examine labor market activities, including the employment or unemployment status, of individuals in the sample. In addition, these data provide interesting insights on the labor market status of potential labor force participants, defined as including all persons between the ages of 14 and 64.

Labor force participation rates derived from this microdata set, shown in Table 3.4, are broadly consistent with the picture obtained from other data sources, with the total labor force participation rate at 60 percent or below, lower participation rates in the center

---

[11]This is potentially an important result. Since larger firms are permitted to link pay levels that are above nationally contracted minimums to firm-specific productivity and profitability, this suggests that labor productivity is, on average, higher in larger firms. This indicates that there could be significant efficiency losses arising from labor market regulations that have fostered an industrial structure that is skewed toward smaller firms.

[12]Bertola and Ichino (1995a) and Erickson and Ichino (1995) examine wage inequality and changes in the Italian wage structure over time. Also see Casavola, Gavosto, and Sestito (1995).

Table 3.3. Wage Regressions for Logarithms of Net Hourly Earnings

	All	Agriculture	Manufacturing	Construction	Trade	Transport and Communications	Finance	Real Estate	Household and Personal Services	Government
Center	-0.06*	-0.07	-0.05*	-0.10	-0.07	0.07	-0.10*	-0.19*	-0.13	-0.03
	(0.01)	(0.16)	(0.02)	(0.06)	(0.04)	(0.07)	(0.05)	(0.09)	(0.07)	(0.02)
South	-0.12*	-0.31*	-0.15*	-0.14*	-0.33*	-0.01	-0.07	-0.37*	-0.27*	-0.01
	(0.01)	(0.12)	(0.02)	(0.05)	(0.03)	(0.06)	(0.05)	(0.09)	(0.06)	(0.02)
High school diploma	0.18*	0.28*	0.17*	0.11*	0.07*	0.31*	0.19*	0.01	0.06	0.22*
	(0.01)	(0.12)	(0.01)	(0.05)	(0.03)	(0.06)	(0.06)	(0.10)	(0.06)	(0.02)
College degree	0.46*	-0.10	0.40*	0.65*	0.39*	0.34*	0.43*	0.09	0.38	0.51*
	(0.02)	(0.46)	(0.04)	(0.17)	(0.09)	(0.12)	(0.07)	(0.14)	(0.21)	(0.02)
Male	0.09*	0.12	0.12*	-0.12	0.07*	0.21*	0.14*	0.14	0.09	0.06*
	(0.01)	(0.09)	(0.02)	(0.09)	(0.03)	(0.08)	(0.05)	(0.08)	(0.06)	(0.01)
Firm size (ii) (20–99)	0.11*	-0.07	0.10*	0.02	0.16*	0.04	0.20*	0.26*	0.17*	...
	(0.02)	(0.13)	(0.02)	(0.05)	(0.04)	(0.09)	(0.08)	(0.10)	(0.07)	
Firm size (iii) (100–499)	0.19*	0.19	0.17*	0.07	0.26*	0.12	0.34*	0.31	0.24*	...
	(0.02)	(0.17)	(0.02)	(0.08)	(0.06)	(0.09)	(0.07)	(0.16)	(0.09)	
Firm size (iv) (over 500)	0.27*	0.41	0.27*	0.12	0.29*	0.27*	0.22*	0.32*	0.33*	...
	(0.02)	(0.46)	(0.02)	(0.09)	(0.05)	(0.07)	(0.05)	(0.14)	(0.11)	
Relative premium	...	-0.05	...	0.01	-0.01	0.09*	0.22*	-0.01	-0.05*	0.31*
	...	(0.03)	...	(0.02)	(0.02)	(0.03)	(0.03)	(0.03)	(0.02)	(0.02)
Adjusted R squared	0.44	0.08	0.41	0.22	0.35	0.32	0.57	0.39	0.17	0.30
Number of observations	6,201	180	1,849	351	667	189	224	178	297	2,266

Sources: Bank of Italy, *Household Survey* (1995); and author's calculations.

Notes: The firm size dummy variables are based on the total number of registered employees (indicated in parentheses) in the establishment. The relative premium is the estimated average sectoral hourly earnings premium relative to the manufacturing sector, expressed as a percentage of average hourly earnings in manufacturing. These premiums were computed from the coefficients on the industry dummies in the regression with "all" observations (column 1). The additional controls included in the regressions are experience and its square, and the following dummy variables: married, urban, invalid, and sick (persons with chronic diseases). An asterisk indicates statistical significance at the 5 percent level.

Table 3.4.   Labor Force Participation Rates
(In percent)

	Italy	North	Center	South
All	58.2	60.8	58.5	55.3
Male	72.5	71.8	72.3	73.4
Female	44.2	49.9	45.4	37.4

Table 3.5.   Reasons for Nonparticipation in Labor Force
(In percent)

	Italy	North	Center	South
Housewives	36.9	30.4	35.2	43.8
Retired on a worker's pension	20.5	29.7	21.4	11.5
Receiving other pensions	7.3	6.0	8.2	8.0
Other (including students)	35.3	33.8	35.3	36.6

and south than in the north, and considerably lower participation rates among women than among men.

One of the survey questions asks for the reasons for nonparticipation in the labor force (Table 3.5). Although the information obtained from the replies is limited, it is nevertheless quite revealing. A substantial proportion of persons between the ages of 14 and 64 who did not consider themselves to be active in the labor force identified themselves as housewives, indicative of the weak attachment of married women to the labor force. There are also marked regional disparities in these data. Married women in the south have a significantly lower participation rate than those in the north. Retired persons on pensions from work constitute about 30 percent of those outside of the labor force in the north but only 12 percent of those in the south.

Next, the data are used to examine the principal activities of labor force participants. Table 3.6 classifies labor force participants into those who have dependent employment, the self-employed, those looking for their first job, and persons who have held jobs in the past but are currently unemployed (in the month of the survey). Overall, about 7 percent of labor force participants considered themselves unemployed, while an additional 10 percent were unemployed and in search of their first job. These figures together indicate an aggregate unemployment rate higher than the official unemployment rate (based on the Labor Force Survey) largely because the latter measure uses a more stringent definition of labor force participation based on job search activity.

Once again, a striking feature of this table is the large discrepancy among regions. In the north only about 8 percent of labor force participants were looking for their first job or were unemployed in 1995. In the center this proportion was about 14 percent, and in the south it reached 30 percent, of which almost two-thirds were first-time job seekers. In the south, the high percentage of labor force participants in search of their first job hints at the inadequacy of mechanisms for the school-to-work transition. In the

north, on the other hand, the proportion of participants looking for their first job was less than 4 percent, indicating the relative tightness of the labor market in that region. The regional disparity of unemployment rates depicted in this table also points to inefficiency in the mechanisms for matching potential workers with available jobs. In particular, public employment agencies have up until now enjoyed a monopoly in providing employment intermediation. These agencies did not provide job listings or other means of matching workers and jobs even across provinces, thereby failing to facilitate the geographical mobility of labor.

Effective mechanisms for absorbing new entrants into the labor force are an important determinant of the efficient functioning of the labor market. The previous set of results indicated that, in this regard, the Italian labor market appears to be inefficient. An examination of unemployment rates among younger workers between the ages of 14 and 25 confirms this and reveals a sizeable youth unemployment rate of about 20 percent in the north and over 60 percent in the south (see Table 3.7). Even those with higher levels of education appear to face high unemployment rates in all regions.[13] This points to a crucial problem with the functioning of the labor market in Italy—the absence of mechanisms to facilitate the school-to-work transition for younger workers. A related hypothesis is that the educational system has not adapted to provide the right set of skills demanded in the labor market, where skill-biased technological change has increased the demand for specialized skills consistent with rapidly improving technology.

---

[13]This result should be viewed with some caution, however, because the number of young college-educated labor force participants in the sample is quite small.

Table 3.6. Current Activities of Labor Force Participants
(In percent)

	Italy	North	Center	South
Dependent employment	62.1	70.7	62.7	51.9
Self-employed	20.6	21.6	23.5	17.9
Looking for first job	10.3	3.7	7.8	19.5
Unemployed	7.0	4.1	6.1	10.7

Table 3.7. Youth Unemployment Rates
(In percent)

	Italy	North	Center	South
All				
Looking for first job	39.7	15.9	34.0	62.0
Other unemployed	7.5	4.9	7.6	9.6
No high school diploma				
Looking for first job	38.4	14.2	29.0	56.2
Other unemployed	10.3	6.8	8.6	12.9
High school diploma or above				
Looking for first job	41.2	17.3	38.0	71.6
Other unemployed	4.4	3.3	6.8	4.3

Another important aspect of unemployment that has been stressed in various contexts is the increasing share of long-term unemployment in total unemployment. This has implications for the persistence of unemployment as well as for social welfare in a broader sense. The long-term unemployed face an attrition of their skills, making them less attractive to prospective employers. Furthermore, the attachment of the long-term unemployed to the labor force tends to weaken over time.

Table 3.8 shows the distribution of unemployment among labor force participants who have experienced only short spells of unemployment (less than six months) and those who have experienced at least one long spell of unemployment (six months or more). Clearly, the contribution of the long-term unemployed to total unemployment is substantial, especially in the south, and indicates the possibility of considerable hysteresis in the unemployment rate.

Determinants of Employment and Labor Force Participation Propensities

To buttress the results discussed above, a more formal empirical analysis of the determinants of employment probabilities and labor force participation propensities is now presented. After narrowing the sample to individuals between the ages of 14 and 64 who identified themselves as labor force participants, employment probit models were estimated in which the employment dummy was regressed on a number of control variables. The results are presented in Table 3.9. The first column contains the results for the full sample, and the next three columns provide results broken down by region (excluding the regional dummies).

For the full sample, estimated employment probabilities are lower in the center and markedly lower in the south relative to the north. An interesting result is that higher education (a college degree) improves

employment probabilities in the south but not in the north. This may simply reflect the relative tightness of the labor market in the north, where there appears to be strong demand for workers of all skill levels. Employment probabilities are higher for males and for married persons. Employment probabilities for married females are not significantly different from those for unmarried females.[14]

Table 3.9 also reports the results of probit regressions that examine the determinants of labor force participation propensities. These propensities are significantly lower in the south than in the north and center. Higher levels of education are clearly associated with higher rates of entry into the labor force. Labor force participation propensities are higher for males than for females in the north and even more strongly so in the south. In addition, these propensities are much lower for married females than for single females. These last two results are indicative of problems in integrating women into the workforce. Thus, it appears that the limited availability of part-time and other flexible work arrangements dissuades women, especially married women, from entering the labor force.

These results suggest that college-educated workers have much higher propensities to enter the labor force than those with lower levels of education, but their employment probabilities, although better, are

---

[14]A further striking result that is not shown here is the substantially lower probability of employment for workers with a history of one or more long spells (six months or longer) of unemployment. This is true in all regions and indicates the employability problems associated with long-term unemployment. The regressions containing this result are not reported here because this variable was available for only a limited subsample.

Table 3.8. Length of Unemployment Spell Among Unemployed
(In percent)

Period	Italy	North	Center	South
Less than six months	17.7	23.2	21.4	13.9
Six months or more	82.3	76.8	78.6	86.1

not very different from those of workers with only a high school diploma. In combination with the large estimated wage premium for employed workers with a college diploma, this suggests that there are mismatches between the types of skills demanded by employers and the average skills acquired through a college education.

The high rate of youth unemployment and the relatively large proportion of young labor market participants looking for their first jobs also indicate some basic problems with the prevailing job matching mechanisms. More fundamentally, they may also indicate a mismatch between the skills emphasized by the educational system and the skills desired by prospective employers. These findings suggest the need for reexamining the focus of the educational system and, from a shorter-term standpoint, providing more job search assistance for younger workers.

Conclusions

The Italian labor market suffers from a number of institutional impediments that have hindered its efficient functioning. Although several reforms have been instituted in recent years, much remains to be done.[15]

The regional segmentation of labor markets remains a major source of inefficiency in the Italian economy. The relatively poor infrastructure in the south and other structural problems in these regions have discouraged investment. Elimination of structural impediments—including inefficient public administration, inadequate infrastructure, and constraints on administering the rule of law—are necessary to stimulate new investment.[16]

Another central concern is the lack of wage differentiation between the north and south. As documented by numerous authors, productivity levels in the south are much lower than in the north while, as shown in this paper, the wage differentials across these regions are relatively narrow.[17] To offset this discrepancy between productivity and wages, which could imply significantly higher unit labor costs in the south, the government has resorted to measures such as reductions in the social security contributions by employers in the south. These measures, however, have a fiscal dimension that is ultimately reflected in other distortionary revenue measures that could affect aggregate economic activity and employment levels.

Recent initiatives to tackle regional disparities include special contracts for depressed areas, such as the *patti territoriali* and *contratti d'area*. These schemes are intended to encourage collaborative efforts by all social partners at the local level in promoting investment and employment creation. For instance, under these initiatives unions have permitted temporary derogations from national wage agreements and have agreed to a greater flexibility of working arrangements. These contracts, although limited in number thus far, appear to have had some success in increasing economic activity in depressed areas. However, such derogations from national wage agreements are intended to be only temporary, and thus may have limited the impact on investment decisions, which typically involve a longer planning horizon.

A more forceful measure would be to restructure wage-bargaining arrangements to allow for regional wage differentiation in line with productivity differentials in a more durable manner. This would enhance the incentives for interregional labor mobility and would simultaneously reduce regional imbalances in the demand for labor by inducing investment flows into high-unemployment areas.

---

[15]The 1970 Charter of Workers' Rights (*Statuto dei Lavoratori*) resulted in substantial rigidities in areas such as hiring and firing procedures, the compensation structure, and the rules for workers' mobility within firms. These rigidities and their deleterious effects are well documented in the literature. See Demekas (1994) and Bertola and Ichino (1995b) for a comprehensive description of labor market institutions in Italy, and Brunetta and Ceci (1996) for details on the 1992–93 tripartite agreement and related reforms. More recent reforms are documented in Prasad and Utili (1998).

[16]Castronuovo (1992) cites evidence that the profitability of investment—measured as the marginal ratio of capital to product—is lower in the south compared to the north.

[17]For instance, Castronuovo (1992) estimates that in the manufacturing sector there was a gap of about 20 percent in labor productivity between the north and south in 1989. Viviani and Vulpes (1995) estimate similar interregional differentials in total factor productivity. Taylor and Bradley (1997) conclude that differentials in unit labor costs across Italian regions are statistically and economically significant determinants of both the levels and persistence of regional disparities in unemployment rates.

Table 3.9. Determinants of Labor Force Status
(Probit estimates)

	Employment				Labor Force Participation			
	Total	North	Center	South	Total	North	Center	South
Center	−0.38*	...	...	...	−0.03	...	...	...
	(0.05)	...	...	...	(0.03)	...	...	...
South	−0.96*	...	...	...	−0.13*	...	...	...
	(0.04)	...	...	...	(0.03)	...	...	...
High school diploma	0.19*	0.14*	0.12	0.23*	0.14*	0.16*	0.12*	0.12*
	(0.04)	(0.07)	(0.08)	(0.06)	(0.03)	(0.04)	(0.06)	(0.04)
College degree	0.15*	−0.05	0.08	0.31*	0.68*	0.52*	0.53*	0.96*
	(0.06)	(0.10)	(0.15)	(0.09)	(0.05)	(0.08)	(0.12)	(0.09)
Male	0.21*	0.37*	0.21*	0.13	0.26*	0.12*	0.15*	0.42*
	(0.05)	(0.08)	(0.10)	(0.07)	(0.03)	(0.06)	(0.08)	(0.05)
Married	0.49*	0.35*	0.51*	0.55*	0.66*	0.55*	0.67*	0.78*
	(0.05)	(0.10)	(0.13)	(0.08)	(0.05)	(0.07)	(0.10)	(0.08)
Married* female	0.13	0.20	−0.02	0.21	−1.42*	−1.28*	−1.53*	−1.59*
	(0.07)	(0.13)	(0.16)	(0.11)	(0.05)	(0.08)	(0.11)	(0.08)
Number of observations	9,971	4,254	2,072	3,645	16,971	6,926	3,514	6,531

Sources: Bank of Italy, *Household Survey* (1995); and author's calculations.

Notes: Additional controls included in the regressions are: experience and its square, and the following dummy variables: urban, invalid, and sick (persons with chronic diseases). An asterisk indicates statistical significance at the 5 percent level.

More generally, intersectoral and interregional labor mobility remain quite low in Italy, reducing the ability of the economy to respond to region- and industry-specific shocks without provoking persistent effects on employment and unemployment.[18] A key deterrent to labor mobility is the lack of wage differentiation across sectors and, as noted, across regions. Allowing for wage contracts that more accurately reflect productivity differentials would enable a more efficient allocation of labor.

Another constraint on labor mobility arises from the ineffectiveness of formal job matching through public employment agencies, which have until recently enjoyed a long-standing monopoly.[19] These agencies apparently provide little assistance in job matching across regions. Furthermore, they have been oriented more toward collecting employment statistics rather than assisting in employment intermediation. Allowing for an expanded role for private sector employment agencies and fostering a greater role for both private and public sector agencies in providing cross-regional job listings would be important steps in improving the efficiency of job matching, both within and across regions.

Removing institutional constraints that impede the efficient operation of labor market adjustment mechanisms could have important welfare implications and could also influence the performance of the Italian economy under EMU.

---

[18]Attanasio and Padoa-Schioppa (1991) and Faini, Galli, Gennari, and Rossi (1997) document the low and declining levels of interregional migration, although these two sets of authors reach different conclusions about the role of income support mechanisms and other institutional factors in influencing such migration.

[19]The *SVIMEZ* report for 1997 indicates that only about 7.5 percent of new job placements in Italy were arranged by public employment agencies. This proportion is substantially lower than in most other European countries, many of which permit the operation of private employment agencies. These include England (about 33 percent), Germany (37 percent), and the Netherlands (63 percent). Faini, Galli, Gennari, and Rossi (1997) cite evidence that informal networks, such as family and friends, play a far more important role in job matching in Italy, especially in the south, than in other countries.

References

Attanasio, Orazio, and Fiorella Padoa-Schioppa, 1991, "Regional Inequalities, Migration, and Mismatch in Italy, 1960–86," in *Mismatch and Labor Mobility,* ed. by Fiorella Padoa-Schioppa (Cambridge: Cambridge University Press), pp. 237–320.

Bayoumi, Tamim, and Eswar S. Prasad, 1997, "Currency Unions, Economic Fluctuations, and Adjustment: Some New Empirical Evidence," *Staff Papers,* International Monetary Fund, Vol. 44 (March), pp. 36–58.

Bertola, Giuseppe, and Andrea Ichino, 1995a, "Wage Inequality and Unemployment: United States vs. Europe," in *NBER Macroeconomics Annual,* ed. by Ben Bernanke and Julio Rotemberg (Cambridge: MIT Press), pp. 13–54.

———, 1995b, "Crossing the River: A Comparative Perspective on Italian Employment Dynamics," *Economic Policy: A European Forum* (October), pp. 359–415.

Brunetta, Renato, and Anna Ceci, 1996, "The Debate on Employment in Italy: Main Topics and Lines for Reform" (unpublished; Rome: Fondazione Giacomo Brodolini).

Calmfors, Lars, and John Driffill, 1988, "Bargaining Structure, Corporatism and Macroeconomic Performance," *Economic Policy,* Vol. 3 (April), pp. 14–61.

Calmfors, Lars, 1993, "Centralization of Wage Bargaining and Economic Performance: A Survey," OECD Economics Studies (Paris: Organization for Economic Cooperation and Development), pp. 161–91.

Casavola, Paola, A. Gavosto, and Paolo Sestito, 1995, "Salari e Mercato Locale del Lavoro," *Lavoro e relazioni industriali,* No. 4.

Castronuovo, Salvatore A., 1992, "Mezzogiorno: The Theory of Growth and the Labor Market," *Journal of Regional Policy,* Vol. 12, pp. 333–65.

Demekas, Dimitri G., 1994, "Labor Market Institutions and Flexibility in Italy: A Critical Evaluation and Some International Comparisons," IMF Working Paper 94/30 (Washington: International Monetary Fund).

Erickson, Christopher, and Andrea Ichino, 1995, "Wage Differentials in Italy: Market Forces, Institutions, and Inflation," in *Differences and Changes in Wage Structures,* ed. by Richard Freeman and Lawrence Katz (Chicago: University of Chicago Press), pp. 265–305.

Faini, Riccardo, Giampaolo Galli, Pietro Gennari, and Fulvio Rossi, 1997, "An Empirical Puzzle: Falling Migration and Growing Unemployment Differentials Among Italian Regions," *European Economic Review,* Vol. 41, pp. 571–79.

Keane, Michael, and Eswar Prasad, 1996, "The Employment and Wage Effects of Oil Price Changes: A Sectoral Analysis," *Review of Economics and Statistics,* Vol. 78 (August), pp. 389–400.

OECD, 1997, *Survey of Italy* (Paris: Organization for Economic Cooperation and Development).

Prasad, Eswar S., and Francesca Utili, 1998, "The Italian Labor Market: Stylized Facts, Institutions, and Directions for Reform," IMF Working Paper 98/42 (Washington: International Monetary Fund).

Pugliese, Enrico, 1993, "Labor Market and Employment Structure in the Mezzogiorno," *Journal of Regional Policy,* Vol. 13, pp. 147–57.

SVIMEZ (Associazione per lo Sviluppo dell'Industria nel Mezzogiorno), 1997, *Rapporto sull'economia del Mezzogiorno.*

Taylor, Jim, and Steve Bradley, 1997, "Unemployment in Europe: A Comparative Analysis of Regional Disparities in Germany, Italy, and the U.K.," *Kyklos,* Vol. 50, pp. 221–45.

Viviani, Carlo, and Giuseppe Vulpes, 1995, "Dualismo Regionale, Divari di Produttività e Infrastrutture," *Rassegna Economica,* Vol. 59 (July–September), pp. 661–88.

IV Regional Labor Markets in Spain

Paolo Mauro and Antonio Spilimbergo

Spain's unemployment rate, at a staggering 21 percent in 1997, is the highest among industrial countries. Similarly striking is the variation of unemployment rates among its 17 regions, ranging from less than 14 percent in the Balearic Islands to more than 32 percent in Andalucía. A finer level of geographical disaggregation is that of the 50 provinces, which are subsets of regions, where unemployment rates vary even more widely, ranging from 8 percent in Lleida, Cataluña, to 36 percent in Jaén, Andalucía (Figure 4.1). Moreover, these differences have persisted for several years and show no signs of abating.

Such large, persistent differences in unemployment rates are considered a problem for three reasons. First, in the early stages of a recovery wage pressures will arise in areas with relatively low unemployment. With limited labor mobility, high unemployment in other areas will not moderate those pressures; higher inflation may soon spread to the whole country, with no commensurate decline in unemployment. In other words, large geographic differences in unemployment rates may cause the nonaccelerating inflation rate of unemployment (NAIRU) to be higher than it would be otherwise. Second, persistent unemployment imbalances constitute evidence that the labor market does not function properly, in that adjustment to past shocks is exceedingly slow. Imbalances also suggest that there may be scope for reducing unemployment in those areas where it is more severe, thereby lowering the nationwide unemployment rate. Third, for a given national unemployment rate, the overall human cost may be higher if the unemployed are not distributed evenly over the country's territory. For example, overall social welfare is lower if one family has two members unemployed and another has both members employed than if both families have only one member unemployed.

This section analyzes the reasons for the persistence of geographical unemployment imbalances and the low speed of adjustment to regional labor demand shocks. It argues that, under present labor market arrangements, these imbalances are unlikely to be corrected in the near future. In particular, the current wage-bargaining system appears to be excessively centralized and results in nationally set wages that are too high to reduce unemployment in high-unemployment areas. To support this claim, this study provides new evidence that there are no significant differences in unit labor costs and real wages between high-unemployment and low-unemployment areas, resulting in muted incentives for firms to migrate and implying that incentives for workers to migrate are only provided by differences in unemployment. The study makes policy suggestions to reduce the NAIRU and promote faster adjustment to regional shocks. The study argues that the wage-bargaining system should be decentralized to the individual firm level. It also suggests a number of measures that are likely to have the greatest impact on low-skilled workers, where the problems are most serious.

Geographic Differences in Unemployment Rates and Their Persistence

In the wide range of unemployment rates among Spanish regions, the distribution patterns are not easy to identify. Generally speaking, southern agricultural regions, such as Andalucía and Extremadura, and some of the northern regions with declining industries, such as País Vasco, Cantabria, and Asturias, tend to have higher unemployment. At the same time, the geographical distribution of unemployment rates in Spain is not as straightforward as in other countries characterized by large regional differences.[1] In Spain, there is no clear north/south divide; there is no simple relationship between unemployment rates and proximity to continental European markets; the sectoral composition of output provides only a partial explanation for unemploy-

---

[1]For instance, the picture in Spain is not as clear as in Italy, where unemployment is higher in the southern regions, which are further from the markets of the rest of Europe, more agricultural, and less prosperous.

Figure 4.1. Unemployment Rates by Province
(1997, second quarter)

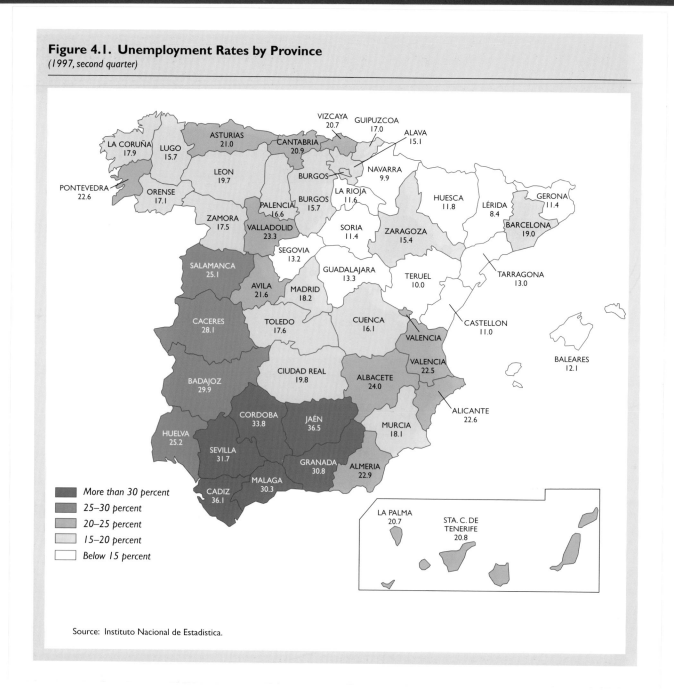

Source: Instituto Nacional de Estadistica.

ment differences; and, perhaps of most interest, the correlation between unemployment rates and GDP per capita and productivity is relatively low.

Even though generalizations may not be easy, it is clear that a regional dimension of the unemployment problem exists: in fact, regional dummies explain individuals' employment status to a significant extent when controlling for personal characteristics such as age, gender, and education. In addition to the large differences among regions, there is also substantial variation in unemployment rates among provinces

within regions. Again, it is difficult to identify clear patterns, but provinces dominated by large cities seem to have somewhat higher unemployment rates than provinces with only small urban centers.

Whatever the determinants of the geographic distribution of unemployment rates, there is compelling evidence that the current pattern has persisted for a long time. The sharp increase in unemployment experienced by the country as a whole since the late 1970s has affected all regions. There have been almost no changes in the regions' unemployment rate rankings, and absolute differences in unemployment rates have widened considerably. Figure 4.2 shows the unemployment rates for Spain's 17 regions and indicates that there are only a few points where lines intersect, and the spread is much wider at the end of the period than at the beginning.

Scatter plots of the average survey unemployment rates in 1980 and 1995 for provinces reveal a remarkable correlation between the provinces with higher unemployment rates today and those that had higher unemployment rates one and a half decades ago (Figure 4.3, top panel).[2] These correlations are much higher in the case of Spain than for the United States and somewhat higher than for other European countries, especially the United Kingdom (Decressin and Fatás, 1995, and Obstfeld and Peri, 1998). These persistent imbalances in unemployment rates constitute prima facie evidence that something is not functioning properly in the Spanish labor market.

There is little doubt that geographic unemployment differences are large and persistent, in spite of uncertainties surrounding the "real" unemployment rate and the size of the underground economy in Spain. At the same time, a brief discussion on the reliability of the data is in order. The most important question in this context is whether high measured unemployment in certain areas might simply reflect a larger underground economy. In that respect, the most widely used measure of unemployment—that based on the National Statistical Institute's survey, which is conducted along internationally accepted guidelines—is judged reliable. Workers in the underground economy are not asked to, nor do they have any incentive to, report themselves as unemployed in the survey. Nevertheless, in light of the extremely high unemployment rate—21 percent for the country as a whole—estimated by the survey, it has been argued that the registered unemployment rate, which amounts only to 13 percent, might be a more reliable measure. In principle, those employed in the underground economy could well register themselves as unemployed, but in practice the checks conducted by the unemployment benefits offices may help reduce this problem. Using registered unemployment data, the same pattern of large and persistent geographic unemployment differences remains quite striking (Figure 4.3, bottom panel). Registered unemployment rates in 1995[3] ranged from 11 percent in Rioja to more than 20 percent in Andalucía among Spain's 17 regions; and from 7

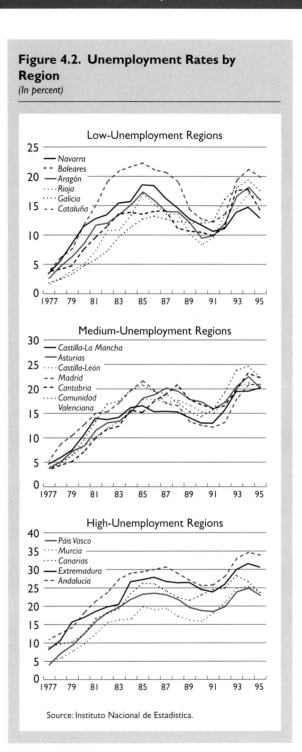

Figure 4.2. Unemployment Rates by Region
(In percent)

Low-Unemployment Regions
— Navarra
- - Baleares
— Aragón
· · Rioja
· · · Galicia
- · Cataluña

Medium-Unemployment Regions
— Castilla-La Mancha
— Asturias
· · · · Castilla-León
- - Madrid
- - Cantabria
- - Comunidad Valenciana

High-Unemployment Regions
— Páis Vasco
· · · · Murcia
· · · · Canarias
— Extremadura
- - Andalucía

Source: Instituto Nacional de Estadística.

percent in Lleida, Cataluña, to 24 percent in Cádiz, Andalucía, among Spain's 50 provinces.

Potential Adjustment Mechanisms

In a well-functioning labor market, one would expect geographical unemployment differences result-

---

[2]The scatter plots are similar in the case of the regions.

[3]Registered unemployment tends to underestimate the geographical differences in unemployment because it excludes the 250,000 people covered by the rural employment program in Extremadura and Andalucía even at times when they are not working, which is often a large proportion of the year.

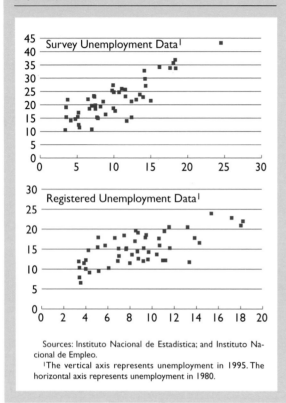

Figure 4.3. Persistence of Unemployment in the Spanish Provinces: Survey Rate and Registered Rate

(In percent)

Sources: Instituto Nacional de Estadística; and Instituto Nacional de Empleo.

[1] The vertical axis represents unemployment in 1995. The horizontal axis represents unemployment in 1980.

ing from past shocks to be reduced, if not altogether eliminated, relatively quickly. Below is a brief description of the potential adjustment mechanisms.

- Migration of firms. Ample availability of unemployed labor in a given area should encourage firms to move there, particularly if widespread and persistent unemployment has reduced wages, and this labor is now cheaper (adjusting for differences in productivity) than elsewhere. This is a relatively unexplored mechanism, owing to the limited availability of information on the migration of firms, but in a well-functioning market it could play a major role in reducing unemployment differences.

- Creation of new jobs by existing or new local firms. Following a decline in labor demand, if lower wages were to result from the new availability of unemployed workers, job creation by existing or new local firms would be encouraged, thereby beginning to reverse the initial decrease in labor demand.

- Changes in the labor force participation rate. When an area is characterized by high and persistent unemployment, it is likely that some unemployed workers will become discouraged and drop out of the labor force. Of course, this is a less desirable way to reduce unemployment than through other mechanisms.

- Migration of workers. When unemployment is very high in a given area, it is reasonable to expect that unemployed workers will migrate to seek jobs elsewhere. Unemployment itself is obviously the most powerful incentive to migrate. However, if a decline in labor demand were to be accompanied not only by higher unemployment but also by a decline in wages, the incentives for the unemployed to leave the area would be even greater. Since this last mechanism played an important role through the 1960s, it is interesting to analyze why it has ceased to do so.

Migration flows, both toward other countries and within Spain, were very large in the 1960s but dropped sharply beginning in the late 1970s. The main reason for this decline is likely to be that absolute unemployment rates rose in the whole country as well as in the rest of Europe. It is well known that workers tend not to migrate—regardless of how bad prospects are in their current location—if the chances of finding a job elsewhere are low. This phenomenon of falling migration at a time of rising absolute unemployment has been well documented not only in the case of Spain (Bentolila, 1997), but also in other countries, including Germany (Decressin, 1994), Italy (Attanasio and Padoa-Schioppa, 1991), and the United Kingdom (Pissarides and McMaster, 1984). The rise of the absolute unemployment rate does not provide a full explanation, however, for the reluctance of labor force participants to move, because less than half of unemployed workers declare they would be willing to fill a vacancy in another region.

In sum, a number of mechanisms may reduce imbalances in unemployment rates, but they have failed to operate in the case of Spain. Among them, wage flexibility plays a key role because declines in wages in high-unemployment areas could spur a sizable migration of firms, although migration of workers may be rather insensitive to wage differentials.

To What Extent Do Wages Adjust?

In spite of large and persistent differences in unemployment, unit labor costs and real wages do not differ much between the high-unemployment and the low-unemployment areas. This is contrary to what one would expect in a well-functioning labor market, one in which wages in areas long bedeviled by high unemployment would normally decline to attract firms and encourage workers to leave, thereby correcting unemployment imbalances.

In addition to large imbalances in unemployment rates among the Spanish regions and provinces, there are also considerable differences in salaries, prices, and productivity in various parts of the country. For example, consider the differences between the province of Barcelona, one of Spain's most economically advanced cities with an unemployment rate of 18 percent, and the province of Badajoz, Extremadura, in the agricultural south with an unemployment rate of 32 percent. Nominal wages are 21 percent higher in Barcelona than in Badajoz, but consumer prices are also 16 percent higher, resulting in a real wage differential of only 5 percent. Productivity is 37 percent higher in Barcelona than in Badajoz, resulting in unit labor costs that are 16 percent lower in the former than in the latter.[4]

The comparison between Barcelona and Badajoz illustrates three simple points. First, there are considerable differences in wages, prices, and productivity, as well as in unemployment rates, among the various parts of the country. Second, even when there are large differences in nominal wages, differences in prices and in productivity may imply that differences in real wages or in unit labor costs are much smaller. In some cases, differences in real wages or in unit labor costs are even of the wrong sign, thereby promoting further geographic divergence in unemployment. Third, differences in unemployment rates do not seem to be closely associated with differences in real wages or unit labor costs, as shown below by more systematic analysis.

A simple, systematic way of analyzing the relationship between unemployment and real wages or unit labor costs is to rank the 50 provinces by their unemployment rate, split the sample in half, and observe cross-sectional averages of the variables for the two groups. Findings based on this procedure and previously unexplored data (see Appendix), indicate that low-unemployment provinces do not have significantly lower real wages or unit labor costs than high-unemployment provinces in either an economic or a statistical sense. This would not be a matter of concern in a country where unemployment rates were fairly uniform or merely temporary; but in a country where unemployment differences are large and persistent, it would be desirable for wages (adjusted for consumer prices

and productivity) to reflect such differences. Lower wages in high-unemployment areas would constitute a helpful market mechanism to correct unemployment imbalances.

Real wages are only marginally higher in the 25 provinces with lower unemployment than in the 25 provinces with higher unemployment because the slightly higher nominal wages are offset to a considerable extent by higher prices (Table 4.1).[5] The real wage differential is insignificant both in an economic and a statistical sense, and is insufficient to encourage workers to move away from high-unemployment provinces.

Unit labor costs are even somewhat lower in provinces with low unemployment because higher productivity more than offsets slightly higher wages. Even though the unit labor cost differential only amounts to 1.53 percent and is not statistically significant, the signal to firms, albeit small, is to move away from high-unemployment areas. Table 4.1 also shows that the same patterns are observed if the analysis is conducted at the regional level.[6] Thus, even though large differences occasionally occur in real wages and unit labor costs among Spanish provinces and regions, these differences are not systematically linked to differences in unemployment rates, and therefore do not foster a correction of unemployment imbalances.[7]

These comparisons of unit labor costs must be interpreted with caution, owing to two types of data limitations. First, the data refer to average, rather than marginal, unit labor costs. The latter are the relevant measure for an entrepreneur choosing where to locate a new firm, and may differ considerably from the former, as in the case of a very modern plant being set up in a relatively backward area. Second, the data refer to overall unit labor costs, rather than to unit labor costs for a particular type of worker in a specific sector.[8] Therefore, significant differences in unit labor costs might exist between high- and low-unemployment areas for certain types of workers and sectors, although these would be offset by opposite differences for other workers and sectors.

---

[4]Higher productivity in Barcelona than in Badajoz may reflect a host of factors, including better infrastructure, a more highly qualified work force, a larger share of advanced sectors in total output, and more modern production plants.

[5]Within price indices, large differences are observed only in the case of housing prices.

[6]These patterns are also observed when national accounts data on the total employee wage bill are used instead of survey data to compute average wages in the various regions, and when value-added data are used instead of gross domestic product data.

[7]Scatter plots and regression analysis also fail to find a close association between unemployment rates and real wages or unit labor costs.

[8]The results are broadly similar when the analysis is conducted on the basis of data for industry only.

Table 4.1   Real Wage and Unit Labor Cost Differentials and Their Sources
(Percent differences between low-unemployment and high-unemployment areas)[1]

	Unemployment Rate[2]	Nominal Wages	Prices	Real Wages	Productivity (GDP per Worker)	Unit Labor Costs	GDP per Person	Employment/ Population Ratio
All 50 provinces (25 low-unemployment vs. 25 high-unemployment provinces)	−10.79	0.49	0.17	0.33	2.06	−1.53	19.81	17.39
	(0.01)	(0.90)	(0.89)	(0.92)	(0.69)	(0.73)	(0.01)	(0.01)
17 provinces with own CPI-level data (8 low-unemployment vs. 9 high-unemployment provinces)	−8.53	9.22	3.89	5.13	12.13	−2.59	26.40	12.73
	(0.01)	(0.18)	(0.05)	(0.40)	(0.09)	(0.69)	(0.01)	(0.01)
All 17 regions (8 low-unemployment vs. 9 high-unemployment regions)	−7.77	1.86	2.01	−0.14	7.19	−4.97	20.54	12.42
	(0.01)	(0.77)	(0.32)	(0.98)	(0.34)	(0.44)	(0.01)	(0.01)

Source: Authors' calculations based on *Instituto Nacional de Estadística* data. See Appendix for details.

[1]The data are 1989–95 averages. There are 17 regions and 50 provinces in Spain. Provinces are subsets of regions. The numbers presented in bold are the differences between the cross-sectional averages for the low-unemployment and high-unemployment groups of provinces and regions. The numbers in parentheses are *p*-values of the test of the null that the two cross-sectional averages are equal. The two groups are defined by ranking the provinces and regions on the basis of the unemployment rate, and splitting the whole sample in half. All averages are geometric, to maintain the approximate validity of the identities: real wages = nominal wages − prices, and unit labor costs = nominal wages − productivity, GDP per person = productivity + employment/population ratio for the average of the differences. CPI-level comparisons across provinces are only available for 17 provinces. Provinces within the same region are assumed to have the same CPI level. Nominal wages are based on survey data.

[2]Difference in percentage points.

The current patterns of real wages and unit labor costs do not bode well for a prompt reduction in geographic unemployment imbalances. In this respect, the situation in Spain bears a striking resemblance to the case of Italy, another country characterized by large imbalances in unemployment rates among its regions. In Italy, the 1996 unemployment rate stood at 22 percent in the south, compared with 8 percent in the north. In the same year, unit labor costs were 2½ percent higher in the south than in the north, implying that firms had an incentive to migrate away from the south. At the same time, the incentives for firms to migrate away from high-unemployment areas are small, and certainly lower than, for example, in Germany, where unit labor costs are about 30 percent higher in the east than in the west despite the fact that the unemployment rate is much higher in the east (18 percent) than in the west (11 percent).

Not only are wage levels too similar in high- and low-unemployment areas to facilitate a correction of imbalances, but there are no significant differences in wage growth rates between high- and low-unemployment provinces, suggesting that there is no tendency for the situation to improve. The average wage increase negotiated over 1992–95 in all agreements between trade unions and entrepreneurs in the 25 provinces with higher unemployment rates was identical to that in the 25 provinces with lower un-

employment rates—both of which amounted to 5.14 percent.[9] This result is consistent with other findings that wage increases do not seem to respond to local labor market conditions.[10]

How Does the Labor Market Adjust to Shocks?

Because of Spain's large and persistent geographic unemployment differences, the labor market adjusts exceedingly slowly to local shocks. This portion of the study analyzes in detail that adjustment process by estimating the extent to which migration takes place, the unemployment rate rises, and the participation rate falls, in response to a drop in labor demand in a given province. It traces these effects through time, comparing the immediate effect with the outcomes observed after a number of years.

---

[9]The cross-sectional standard deviation of the 1992–95 average wage increase settlements for the 50 provinces amounted to 0.27 of a percentage point. The data refer to wage increase settlements reported to the Ministry of Labor, which includes the vast majority of agreements signed by trade unions and employers.

[10]Using data on wages from national accounts at the regional/sectoral level, Bentolila and Jimeno (1995) confirm that wages do not respond to regional unemployment rates, although they respond somewhat to productivity.

The questions above are addressed by estimating a vector autoregression system (VAR) of employment growth, the employment rate, and labor force participation for the 50 Spanish provinces over 1964–92. The framework adopted is identical to that developed by Blanchard and Katz (1992), who first applied it to the United States, and similar to that applied by Decressin and Fatás (1995) to Europe, and Bentolila and Jimeno (1995) to the 17 Spanish regions on quarterly data for 1976–94. As a consequence, the results obtained can be compared with those of the foregoing studies.[11]

The system is the following:

Employment growth:

$$e_{it} = \alpha_{i1} + \beta_1 (L) \Delta e_{it-1} + \gamma_1 (L) le_{it-1}$$
$$+ \delta_1 (L) lp_{it-1} + \in_{iet}; \qquad (4.1)$$

Employment rate:

$$le_{it} = \alpha_{i2} + \beta_2 (L) \Delta e_{it} + \gamma_2 (L) le_{it-1}$$
$$+ \delta_2 (L) lp_{it-1} + \in_{iut}; \qquad (4.2)$$

Labor force participation rate:

$$lp_{it} = \alpha_{i3} + \beta_3 (L) \Delta e_{it} + \gamma_3 (L) le_{it-1}$$
$$+ \delta_3 (L) lp_{it-1} + \in_{ipt}, \qquad (4.3)$$

where all variables are differences between province I and the national average in order to focus on developments at the provincial level that are not the result of nationwide developments: Δe_{it} is the first difference of the logarithm of employment; le_{it} is the logarithm of the ratio of employment to the labor force; and lp_{it} is the logarithm of the ratio of the labor force to the working age population. There are two lags for each right-hand side variable to allow for feedback effects from labor force participation and the employment rate to employment growth. For example, a decrease in labor force participation could lower wages, thereby facilitating an increase in employment growth. The system is estimated by pooling all observations, while allowing for different province-specific constant terms in each equation, because some provinces may have higher average employment growth, employment rates, and labor force participation rates than others for reasons that are not captured by the explanatory variables.

The effects of a fall in employment can be traced through time by analyzing the impulse response graphs based upon the estimated parameters of the system above. Those effects can be interpreted as resulting from a decline in labor demand, under the reasonable assumption that most of the year-to-year changes in employment reflect changes in labor demand, rather than labor supply.[12]

The immediate response to a decline in labor demand in a given Spanish province does not differ much from that observed in other countries, although the effects on labor participation are greater in some cases. In response to a one percentage point negative shock to employment growth, the unemployment rate immediately increases by 0.31 of a percentage point, while the participation rate decreases by 0.65 of a percentage point (Figure 4.4). The remaining adjustment to the fall in employment is accounted for by migration. The simultaneous effect on the unemployment rate is similar to that estimated by existing studies for both the United States and Europe. The immediate response of the participation rate is similar to that observed in Europe but much higher in Spain than in the United States, suggesting that the phenomenon of the "discouraged worker" plays a larger role in the former than in the latter.

There are more important differences between Spain and other countries in the extent and composition of adjustment to a negative employment shock after several years. In the case of Spain, migration is not sufficient to bring the unemployment rate back to its preshock level even after more than a decade. The participation rate rises back to its preshock level, which it reaches after ten years. These results contrast sharply with those obtained by other studies for both the United States and the rest of Europe, where unemployment rates return to their preshock levels after about five years. In the United States, adverse employment shocks result in a relatively small decline in the participation rate, a small increase in the unemployment rate, and rapid migration in the first few years. After about five years, both the participation rate and the unemployment rate are back at their preshock levels, and employment remains permanently at or below the level attained through the initial shock, with migration being entirely responsible for full adjustment. In the rest of Europe, the overall pattern of the response to an adverse employment shock is fairly similar to that observed in

---

[11]The specification of the VAR system follows exactly Blanchard and Katz (1992) to permit an international comparison of the results. Nevertheless, a number of alternative specifications were estimated to show that the results are robust to specification changes. The results are broadly similar if the system is estimated by using differences rather than levels of the employment rate, or differences of employment growth and levels of the other two variables. The results are very similar if three or four lags of all the variables are used, instead of two lags.

---

[12]Formally, the identifying assumption is that $\in_{iet}$ can be interpreted as an innovation in local labor demand. Correspondingly, current innovations in local employment growth are allowed to affect local employment rates and local participation rates, but not vice versa.

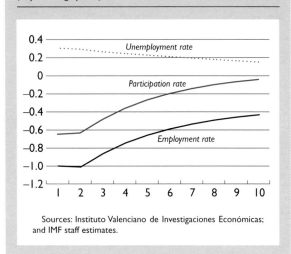

Figure 4.4. Response to a One Percent Negative Employment Shock in a Given Province
(In percentage points)

Sources: Instituto Valenciano de Investigaciones Económicas; and IMF staff estimates.

the United States, although the effects on the participation rate and the unemployment rate are much larger in Europe during the first few years because migration is more sluggish than in the United States.

The analysis conducted above does not distinguish among different educational groups. Mauro and Spilimbergo (1999) find that highly skilled workers migrate very quickly in response to a decline in regional labor demand, whereas the low-skilled workers drop out of the labor force or stayed unemployed. This suggests that labor market adjustment is particularly sluggish among the low skilled.

Current Arrangements That Hinder Labor Market Adjustment

The empirical analysis above shows that the labor market adjusts exceedingly slowly to shocks and geographical imbalances in unemployment. This portion of the study examines those current policies and arrangements that prevent rapid adjustment to shocks. It also relates each of these features of the labor market to the groups of workers, skilled versus unskilled, that they seem to affect the most.

The key barrier to the reduction of existing geographical unemployment differences and the prompt adjustment to local labor demand shocks seems to be the current wage-bargaining system. This barrier affects labor force participants of all groups. A number of other current labor market policies and arrangements hamper the mobility of the low skilled, al-

though probably not that of other groups. These include programs to help agricultural workers in specific depressed areas, such as Andalucía and Extremadura; minimum wage legislation; and the unemployment benefit system. Finally, a number of current policies and aspects of the housing market and in goods and other factor markets also hamper labor market adjustment for workers of all skill levels.

Labor Market Policies and Institutions

The Collective Bargaining System

The collective bargaining system, which covers the majority of workers and firms,[13] plays an important role in preventing wages from falling sufficiently in areas with high unemployment. Information on exactly how many workers are covered by each type of bargaining arrangement is scarce, but perhaps the most representative type of arrangement is one in which a given economic sector, such as banking, has its own national round followed by regional and/or provincial rounds. By international standards, the bargaining system in Spain is considered to have an intermediate degree of centralization (Box 4.1).

On the surface, the complex patchwork of national, regional, provincial, and firm-level negotiations might appear to provide ample scope for geographic flexibility of wages, particularly when one considers that, measured by number of workers, more than half of the agreements signed are at the provincial level (Table 4.2). Also, there appears to be consensus that the number of bargaining units is excessive. Bargaining takes place according to a cascading system, however, in which the outcome of agreements at the broader levels are de facto accepted as minimum standards for the narrower levels. For example, nationwide sectoral agreements set wage floors that are binding on all firms in the sector. The labor market reform of 1994 made it possible for a firm to opt out of these agreements, although only in cases where its economic viability would be endangered by applying the sectoral wage increase, and with the mutual consent of the employer and workers. Not surprisingly, this option has been exercised very seldom. In any case, only about 10 percent of wage earners are covered by firm-level

---

[13]Collective agreements are legally enforceable and apply to all workers in a given firm whether they are unionized or not. It is estimated that about three-fourths of firms and workers are covered by collective bargaining agreements, even though the workers' unionization rate of 10–15 percent is low by international standards.

Box 4.1. The Effects of Bargaining Centralization

Theory and Cross-Country Studies. In a seminal study that initiated a burgeoning literature, Calmfors and Driffill (1988) argued that a fully centralized national bargaining system, or a fully decentralized system with wage setting at the level of the individual firm, was better than an intermediate system in which negotiations took place at the national/sectoral level. To support their claim, they presented empirical cross-country evidence of a hump-shaped relationship between countries' degrees of bargaining centralization and their macroeconomic performance (the latter measured by nationwide unemployment and inflation outcomes). The rationale for that empirical observation, they argued, was that negotiators at the national/sectoral level attempted to raise relative wages for their sector without taking into account the negative external effects in terms of higher national wages that they imposed on other sectors. An additional argument is that nationwide trade unions and entrepreneurs' associations may play a helpful role in containing wages as a part of disinflation programs. By contrast, firm-level negotiations yielded free market outcomes, and negotiators at the economywide level internalized effects on all sectors.

Spain is usually considered to have an intermediate degree of bargaining centralization (Layard, Nickell, and Jackman, 1991). Given the large differences in unemployment rates among the various areas of the country, Spain might benefit from opting for a fully decentralized wage-bargaining system. Under that system, it would be possible for wages to fall in high-unemployment areas, thereby fostering the creation of more jobs in those areas. Such decentralization becomes even more important as Spain enters EMU and consolidates its low-inflation regime, where relative price adjustment may become more difficult.

The Experience of the United Kingdom. At the beginning of the 1980s, the United Kingdom was also characterized by sharp differences in unemployment rates between its northern regions, which suffered from the decline of manufacturing industry, and its southern regions, which managed to create new jobs in the services sector. In 1980–84, the United Kingdom undertook a comprehensive and in-depth labor market reform, which effectively decentralized the wage-bargaining system from the industry or regional level to the firm level. Regional differences in unemployment have fallen sharply since then. For example, the unemployment rate dropped to 8 percent in 1997 from 15 percent in 1984 in the north of England, whereas it declined more slightly in the southeast of England, to 6 percent in 1997 from 8 percent in 1984. However, it remains uncertain whether that decentralization played an important role, especially because it was accompanied by other measures; the reforms may not have eliminated insider power (Ramaswamy and Prasad, 1994); and wages may still fail to respond to local conditions because large firms pay uniform wages to their employees, regardless of the geographic location of their various plants (Walsh and Brown, 1990).

---

agreements, while about 65 percent are covered by industry-wide agreements.[14]

In addition, to the extent that there is scope for wage flexibility, the bargaining parties may have chosen not to use it to its full extent. The two main trade union confederations, *Unión General de Trabajadores* and *Comisiones Obreras,* may have pursued a strategy of "equal work, equal pay," resulting in a low dispersion of wage-rate increases, even since 1986 when the last economywide wage agreement was signed. Employers may have chosen to accommodate this strategy to preserve social peace and to adopt more capital-intensive technologies.

The April 1997 agreement between trade unions and entrepreneurs does not explicitly call for a change in the degree of centralization of the bargaining system, but its implementation could provide the opportunity to make improvements in that area. The

social partners agreed in principle to examine ways of streamlining the bargaining system. Their main concern is that, at present, the same aspects of a contract, for example, working conditions and wages, are often negotiated at several levels of bargaining—national/sectoral, provincial/sectoral, and firm-level—which leads to duplication of effort and confusion. The agreement lends itself to various interpretations, but one positive aspect is that it stipulates that negotiations on wages can take place at the firm level.

Programs to Help Workers in Depressed Areas

Programs to help workers in depressed areas reduce incentives for these workers to accept lower wages (thereby attracting new firms) or to seek jobs elsewhere. An example is the agricultural employment plan, *Plan de Empleo Rural,* which provides farm workers in Andalucía and Extremadura with temporary jobs in state-financed infrastructure projects and unemployment assistance for a substantial portion of the remainder of the year. Under that program, which covers about 250,000 workers and

---

[14]This is an approximation because the data from the Ministry of Labor refer to all agreements, with no information on which workers are covered by more than one agreement, as is very often the case.

Table 4.2. Wage Agreements by Type, 1995
(In percent of total)

	Agreements	Firms	Workers
Total agreements	100.00	100.00	100.00
Firm-level agreements	72.01	0.35	13.61
Firms in one province	62.62	0.31	6.17
Firms in one region	1.75	0.01	0.76
Firms in more than			
one region	7.64	0.04	6.68
Higher-level agreements	27.99	99.65	86.39
Sectoral	26.71	99.63	86.05
Within a province	24.52	78.24	55.25
Within a region	0.55	4.54	2.65
In more than one			
region	0.09	0.11	0.14
Nationwide	1.55	16.74	28.01
Nonsectoral	1.28	0.02	0.34
Within a province	0.99	0.01	0.14
Within a region	0.09	0.00	0.03
In more than one			
region	0.20	0.00	0.17

Source: Ministry of Labor, *Anuario de Estadísticas Laborales y de Asuntos Sociales* (1995).

low end of the pay scale. Its importance in determining labor force participants' willingness to take up jobs is increased by the fact that it affects the level of unemployment assistance and the ceiling and floor for unemployment benefits. Moreover, Spain's minimum wage is applied nationwide, with no adjustments for differences in the cost of living in the various areas of the country. While this institutional feature of the labor market is probably of little consequence for the highly skilled, it may have important consequences for the low skilled, particularly in areas where productivity and the cost of living are low.

The Unemployment Benefit/Assistance Systems

Spain's unemployment benefits system is fairly generous by international standards, though not sufficiently so to explain why Spain's unemployment rate is higher than in other countries.[17] Gross replacement rates are higher than the EU average in the first month of unemployment, and net replacement rates are close to the EU average in the first month, but below the EU average in the sixtieth month of unemployment. The duration of unemployment benefits is equal to one-third of the last job's tenure, up to a maximum of two years;[18] therefore, it does not stand out compared with other countries. Benefits amount to 70 percent of the previous wage for the first 6 months and 60 percent thereafter, with a floor of 75–100 percent of the minimum wage and a ceiling of 170–220 percent, depending on the number of children. Once eligibility for unemployment benefits expires, workers are entitled to means-tested unemployment assistance for another 3–30 months, depending on age, number of years' work prior to dismissal, and number of children, which amounts to 75 percent of the statutory minimum wage. The Spanish unemployment compensation system is rendered particularly generous by the possibility of cumulating unemployment benefits paid by the state with generous dismissal benefits paid by the employer.[19]

Unemployment protection reduces job search efforts by unemployed workers and raises the partici-

accounts for about 5 percent of total expenditure on unemployment benefits in Spain, as few as 40 days of work a year entitle workers to 75 percent of the statutory minimum wage for 40–360 days a year, depending on their age. This program reduces workers' willingness to migrate or to take low-paying jobs in sectors other than agriculture and represents an institutional barrier to labor market adjustment with important consequences to the low-skilled workers in the regions where it is available.

Minimum Wage Legislation

Spain's statutory minimum wage, currently at 32 percent of the average adult wage,[15] is not high by international standards.[16] Nevertheless, it may play some role in preventing wages from falling sufficiently to encourage the creation of new jobs at the

---

[15]This rate declined gradually from 40 percent in 1985. Workers of age 18 and under who are employed under training contracts may be paid 85 percent of the statutory minimum wage.

[16]It is well below the average for EU countries that have a statutory minimum wage (more than 50 percent of the average adult wage). It is also below the average of the minimum wages set through collective agreements in EU countries that do not have a statutory minimum wage.

---

[17]In particular, a thorough comparison between the unemployment benefit systems and other labor market institutions in Spain and Portugal reveals that the differences between these two countries are rather limited, raising the puzzling question of why unemployment is so much worse in the former than in the latter.

[18]A worker must have been employed for at least 12 months in the past 6 years to be eligible for unemployment benefits.

[19]Permanent workers hired before May 1997 typically receive their full salary for 45 days per year worked, up to a maximum of 42 weeks, if they are dismissed for "unjustified" economic causes, which tends to be the majority of cases.

pation rate, thereby contributing to high unemployment and low labor mobility. Antolín and Bover (1997) find that, after controlling for personal characteristics, the unregistered unemployed, who do not receive unemployment benefits, are more mobile than the employed and the registered unemployed. Such adverse effects are particularly harsh on the low-skilled workers because benefits are capped. One positive feature of the current design of Spain's unemployment benefits system is that benefits are determined as a percentage of the previous wage. Therefore, if policy measures, such as the decentralization of the wage-bargaining system, were to be undertaken and resulted in lower wages in high-unemployment areas, unemployment benefits in those areas would fall correspondingly.

Housing Market Arrangements

Current arrangements in the housing market also contribute to limiting the geographic mobility of labor. In particular, the market for rental housing is relatively undeveled and illiquid in Spain, with more than three-fourths of the population living in owner-occupied housing, compared with about 60 percent in a sample of more than 20 OECD countries (Oswald, 1996). The most striking restriction is that the minimum duration of a rental contract is five years. Illiquid rental markets make it difficult for workers to move, especially the less affluent groups of workers, that is, typically the low skilled.[20]

Policies and Institutions in Goods and Other Factor Markets

While it is difficult to assess the flexibility of goods markets and the degree of capital mobility in Spain relative to other countries, some current institutional obstacles seem to be important. To take just one example, it is often difficult to obtain permits to open a new large retail outlet. Such rigidities in goods and factor markets also influence the speed of adjustment to labor demand shocks. For instance, suppose that the demand for labor drops in a given region, and wages fall as a result. Lower wages might attract new firms to that area, but if there are institutional obstacles to such a move, as in the case of large retail outlets, adjustment to the initial shock will take a long time.

---

[20]On the basis of cross-country regressions, Oswald (1996) has suggested that undeveloped markets for rental housing may contribute to higher unemployment rates because workers find it more difficult to move to a new location where jobs might be available. However, his findings may result from the fact that high unemployment reduces migration, implying that a higher share of the population lives in owner-occupied housing.

Conclusions

There are large and persistent differences in unemployment rates among Spanish regions, and there are no signs that these differences can be reduced in the near future under current policies and arrangements. Labor market adjustment to shocks is sluggish, especially among the low skilled. This study has identified a number of measures that would facilitate the reduction of unemployment in depressed regions and foster the speedy adjustment to shocks.

Reforms in several labor market institutions would make it easier for the labor market to respond to shocks and for unemployment differences to be corrected rapidly. The most important reform would be the decentralization of the wage-bargaining system to permit wages to fall in high-unemployment areas, thereby attracting firms and providing an additional incentive for the unemployed to migrate. This measure would benefit workers of all skill levels. Such a reform could only be undertaken with the consensus of the social partners who would have to implement it. Decentralization of the wage-bargaining system becomes even more urgent as Spain joins EMU and consolidates its low-inflation environment, where relative wage adjustment may become more difficult.

To permit a better-informed choice of policies for reforming the wage-bargaining system, it is necessary to establish exactly its current degree of centralization, for example, by estimating more precisely the proportion of wage settlements that are affected by negotiations at the national level. To that end, the trade unions and the entrepreneurs' associations should undertake a census of bargaining practices in Spain—a project that is needed in any case if the social partners wish to implement effectively their agreement in principle to streamline the bargaining system.

Other measures to reform the labor market may be initiated by the government and can have significant effects among the low skilled, where the problem is the worst, even if they have little impact on the high skilled. To provide the right incentives for people to take up employment, it would be desirable to eliminate programs that help workers in specific sectors in depressed areas, continue reducing the minimum wage as a ratio of the average wage, and further tighten the eligibility for unemployment benefits. These actions could be combined with targeted social welfare programs to protect the truly needy sections of the population.

Enhanced competition in other goods and factor markets would also help speed up the adjustment to new labor market shocks and the correction of past shocks, thereby contributing to the reduction of geographic unemployment differentials. In particular, liberalization should be undertaken in the housing market, especially at the low end where restrictions are higher and where benefits to the low skilled would be greatest. Finally, the evidence presented in this study provides an additional argument in favor of improving the educational level of the workforce.

A decentralization of the wage-bargaining system, combined with the other aforementioned measures, would lead to a considerable decline in wages in Spain's high-unemployment areas, with a corresponding decline in unit labor costs. Entrepreneurs would exploit this opportunity by setting up new firms in those areas, causing employment to increase. Eventually, unit labor cost differences would disappear, but in the meantime unemployment differences would be reduced as well.

Appendix: Data Sets on the Spanish Provinces

This section uses a number of relatively unexplored data sets on the Spanish provinces, including those on nominal wages, prices, and productivity; on wage settlements by province; and on population, labor force, and employment by province.

The data on employment, labor force, and working age (16–65) population by province for 1964–92 are drawn from M. Mas, F. Pérez, E. Uriel, and L. Serrano, *Capital Humano, Series Históricas, 1964–1992,* Fundación Bancaja, Spain (1995). This is a unique data set, in that nothing comparable to it exists for other countries. It provides working-age population, as well as active population, and employment data for the 50 Spanish provinces. The results are based on a very comprehensive data collection project conducted by the *Instituto Valenciano de Investigaciones Económicas* (IVIE). Since 1977, the basic source of information used for the project is the individual replies to the labor force survey by the *Instituto Nacional de Estadística* (INE).

Nominal wages data for 1989–95, which are published only by region, were supplied by province by Mr. Miguel Angel de Castro of the INE for this project.

The data on relative prices at a given point in time are only available by region and were drawn from the *Encuesta Regional de Precios 1989,* supplied by the INE. The data for 1989–95 by province were constructed using the provincial price indices relative (time-series) to 1990=100, assuming as a starting point for each province the relative (cross-sectional) price index in 1989.

Data on productivity by province for 1989–95 are drawn from *Contabilidad Regional de España 1989–1995,* INE.

The data on wage settlements by province, for 1992–95, are drawn from *Anuario de Estadísticas Laborales,* Ministerio de Trabajo, Madrid, Spain (various issues). They refer to the average of all wage settlements reported to the Labor Ministry.

References

Antolín, Pablo, and Olympia Bover, 1997, "Regional Migration in Spain: The Effect of Personal Characteristics and of Unemployment, Wage and House Pricing Differentials Using Pooled Cross-Sections," *Oxford Bulletin of Economics and Statistics,* Vol. 59 (May), pp. 215–35.

Attanasio, Orazio, and Fiorella Padoa-Schioppa, 1991, "Regional Inequalities, Migration and Mismatch in Italy," in *Mismatch and Labor Mobility,* ed. by Fiorella Padoa-Schioppa (Cambridge: Cambridge University Press), pp. 237–320.

Bentolila, Samuel, 1997, "La Inmovilidad del Trabajo en las Regiones Españolas," *Papeles de Economía Española,* Vol. 72, pp. 168–77.

Bentolila, Samuel, and Juan Jimeno, 1995, "Regional Unemployment Persistence (Spain, 1976–94)," CEPR Discussion Paper No. 1259 (London: Center for Economic Policy Research).

Blanchard, Olivier-Jean, and Lawrence Katz, 1992, "Regional Evolutions," *Brookings Papers on Economic Activity*:1, Brookings Institution, pp. 1–61.

Calmfors, Lars, and John Driffill, 1988, "Bargaining Structure, Corporatism, and Macroeconomic Performance," *Economic Policy,* Vol. 3 (April), pp. 14–61.

Decressin, Jörg, 1994, "Internal Migration in West Germany and Implications for East-West Salary Convergence," *Weltwirtschaftliches Archiv,* Vol. 130, pp. 231–57.

Decressin, Jörg, and Antonio Fatás, 1995, "Regional Labor Market Dynamics in Europe," *European Economic Review,* Vol. 39 (December), pp. 1627–55.

Layard, Richard, Stephen Nickell, and Richard Jackman, 1991, *Unemployment: Macroeconomic Performance and the Labor Market* (London: Oxford University Press).

Mauro, Paolo, and Antonio Spilimbergo, 1999, "How Do the Skilled and the Unskilled Respond to Regional Shocks? The Case of Spain," *Staff Papers,* International Monetary Fund, Vol. 46 (March), pp. 1–17.

Obstfeld, Maurice, and Giovanni Peri, 1998, "Asymmetric Shocks," *Economic Policy,* Vol. 26 (April), pp. 205–47.

Oswald, Andrew, 1996, "A Conjecture on the Explanation for High Unemployment in the Industrialized Nations," Warwick Economic Research Papers No. 475 (Coventry: University of Warwick).

Pissarides, C. A., and I. McMaster, 1984, "Regional Migration, Wages and Unemployment: Empirical Evidence and Implications for Policy," Centre for Labour Economics Discussion Paper No. 204 (London: London School of Economics).

Ramaswamy, Ramana, and Eswar Prasad, 1994, "Shocks and Structural Breaks: Labor Market Reforms in the United Kingdom," IMF Working Paper 94/152 (Washington: International Monetary Fund).

Walsh, Janet, and William Brown, 1990, "Regional Earnings and Pay Flexibility," Department of Applied Economics Working Paper No. 9008 (Cambridge: University of Cambridge).

V Policy Implications

Paolo Mauro, Eswar Prasad, and Antonio Spilimbergo

The international evidence presented in Section II shows that several European countries are characterized not only by high nationwide unemployment, but also by large differences in regional unemployment. Moreover, such differences have persisted for many years. Both Italy and Spain rank high in terms of these undesirable characteristics. A key policy question in these countries is how to promote the movement of capital toward high-unemployment regions—the adjustment mechanism that could play the main role in correcting regional unemployment imbalances—as well as the movement of labor toward low-unemployment regions.[1] Using data sets and methodologies that are best suited to each country, the two case studies in Sections III and IV yield consistent, complementary results that point to the following policy implications.

The wage-bargaining system is de facto excessively centralized in both countries. As a result, wages in areas that have experienced persistently high unemployment cannot decline sufficiently in relation to those in low-unemployment areas to correct unemployment imbalances. In fact, the study on Italy finds that wages are similar in high-unemployment and low-unemployment regions, controlling for a number of demographic and educational characteristics of the workers; and the study on Spain finds that both real wages and unit labor costs are similar in high-unemployment and low-unemployment regions or provinces. These findings provide an argument in favor of decentralizing the wage-bargaining system to the firm level, so as to allow market forces to bid wages down in the high-unemployment areas.[2] Lower unit labor costs would then attract new firms into the high-unemployment areas; in addition, lower real wages would constitute a further incentive for workers to migrate out of these areas.[3]

Other labor market institutions and policies that tend to set an artificial floor on wages, thereby hampering the creation of new jobs in high-unemployment areas, include minimum wages and unemployment benefits. The floor set by the minimum wage is likely to have adverse consequences for low-skilled labor force participants in areas where productivity is low, that is, typically areas characterized by high unemployment, although it probably does not constitute a binding constraint on wage setting for most other workers in Italy or Spain.[4] Similarly, unemployment benefits tend to reduce job search efforts by the unemployed and to limit downward pressure on wages in areas where unemployment is high. Again, this consideration is more likely to be valid for the low skilled in low-productivity areas. A reduction—or at least the introduction of regional differentiation—in minimum wages and a tightening of eligibility for unemployment compensation could therefore help reduce geographic unemployment differences. These actions could be combined with targeted social welfare programs to protect the truly needy sections of the population.

Special unemployment protection programs often distort incentives, thereby perpetuating regional unemployment differences. The most striking illustration of this is Spain's special unemployment benefit program for temporary agricultural workers in certain depressed areas. This program tends to tie underemployed workers not only to a particular area but also to a certain sector where labor demand is

---

[1]The rate of migration also reflects cultural differences across countries, thus Europe could have a significantly lower rate of migration than the United States even with the same economic incentives. For a study on the importance of cultural attitudes versus economic incentives, see Spilimbergo and Ubeda (1996).

[2]Calmfors and Driffill (1988) argue that both highly centralized and highly decentralized wage-bargaining systems perform better than systems with an intermediate degree of centralization, such as those in Italy and Spain. Their arguments, combined with the considerations above, reinforce the need to move to a highly decentralized system.

[3]Hanson and Spilimbergo (forthcoming) find that international migration between Mexico and the United States is highly sensitive to variations in wage differentials even at a monthly frequency and in the presence of border enforcement.

[4]In Spain, the statutory nationwide minimum wage amounts to one-third of average wages for adults. The minimum wage for workers below 18 years of age with training contracts amounts to 85 percent of the minimum wage for adults. In Italy, there is no statutory minimum wage, but the minimum wages set in collective agreements typically amount to 70 percent of the average wage, a higher percentage than in most other European countries.

unlikely to rise in the future. The elimination of such programs and their replacement with standard unemployment protection could therefore alleviate regional unemployment dispersion.

Lack of flexibility in the housing market also appears to hamper migration of workers. Restrictions often take the form of high transaction costs (including through taxation) on the purchase and sale of residential real estate, long minimum duration of rental contracts, as well as widespread rent control and public allocation of rental housing.[5]

The relative inefficiency of formal labor market intermediation mechanisms in facilitating job matching between employers in low-unemployment regions and labor force participants in high-unemployment regions also limits migration. This has been the case in Italy, where formal job intermediation has been restricted to public sector employment agencies that have proved ineffectual at providing cross-regional job listings. In Spain, the statutory monopoly of job placement held by the National Employment Institute (INEM) was abolished and the establishment of nonprofit private agencies permitted in 1994. In both countries, the private sector should be allowed to play a much greater role in job matching.

Efforts to improve schooling and retrain workers, particularly in areas with higher unemployment, would also help correct unemployment imbalances. Higher education is usually associated with lower unemployment. Some of the areas in Italy and Spain that are characterized by higher unemployment rates also rank among the worst in terms of levels of education achieved. Moreover, the evidence from Spain suggests that workers with higher education migrate more promptly in response to shocks in regional labor demand.

Among the possible instruments that this paper has not analyzed in detail, active regional policy, such as government-provided infrastructure, may be the one currently used to the greatest extent, both at the national level and at the EU level. One example is the structural funds provided to regions whose per capita GDP is below 75 percent of the EU average. In principle, active regional policy could help raise productivity in the high-unemployment areas, thereby making them a more attractive location for firms. At the implementation stage, however, it is often difficult to pick the right sectors or the right type of infrastructure. For example, Italy's active regional policy between the early 1960s and the mid-

1970s, when large-scale industrial plants were built in the south, failed to engender commensurate spillovers in terms of output and employment. Although an analysis of such policies lies outside the scope of this paper, past experience does not bode well for future attempts in this area.

Finally, regional policies should be consistent over time. Both workers and capital make location decisions based on long-term horizons. For this reason, effective regional policies should guarantee stability over time because temporary measures are likely to have negligible effects. In the context of wage-bargaining decentralization, for instance, long-lasting measures are likely to be more effective. The *patti territoriali* and *contratti d'area,* recently introduced in Italy to permit temporary derogations from national wage contracts, have failed to promote the migration of firms to high-unemployment areas partly because they are perceived as providing only temporary wage flexibility.

In addition to policies that could be implemented at the national level, the country studies also provide two key lessons for the euro area as a whole. First, the studies emphasize the importance of relative wage flexibility to correct unemployment imbalances. The expectation that the euro area will be characterized by a low-inflation regime, which—while obviously desirable—will tend to hinder relative wage adjustment, strengthens the case for the policy measures recommended above. Second, a decentralized wage-bargaining system is even more crucial in the euro area, in light of large productivity differences across countries. Calls for "equal work, equal pay" by workers in low-productivity countries, which could well arise once the common currency facilitates comparison of wage levels among euro countries, would tend to lead to higher unemployment in low-productivity countries. The creation of a Europeanwide wage-bargaining system would hamper the ability of individual countries to respond to asymmetric shocks.

References

Calmfors, Lars, and John Driffill, 1988, "Bargaining Structure, Corporatism, and Macroeconomic Performance," *Economic Policy,* Vol. 3 (April), pp. 14–61.

Hanson, Gordon, and Antonio Spilimbergo, forthcoming, "Illegal Immigration, Border Enforcement, and Relative Wages: Evidence from Apprehensions at the U.S.-Mexico Border," *American Economic Review.*

Oswald, Andrew, 1998, "A Conjecture on the Explanation for High Unemployment in the Industrialized Nations," Economic Research Papers No. 475 (University of Warwick).

Spilimbergo, Antonio, and Luis Ubeda, 1996, "Multiple Equilibria in Geographic Labor Mobility" (Ph.D. dissertation; Cambridge, Massachusetts: Massachusetts Institute of Technology).

---

[5]While it is difficult to compare restrictions across countries, the high share of owner-occupation in the total populations of Italy and Spain—70 percent and 75 percent, respectively—compared with about 60 percent in a sample of more than 20 OECD countries (Oswald, 1998)—is an indication that rental market restrictions are relatively stringent in these countries.

Recent Occasional Papers of the International Monetary Fund

177. Perspectives on Regional Unemployment in Europe, by Paolo Mauro, Eswar Prasad, and Antonio Spilimbergo. 1999.

176. Back to the Future: Postwar Reconstruction and Stabilization in Lebanon, edited by Sena Eken and Thomas Helbling. 1999.

175. Macroeconomic Developments in the Baltics, Russia, and Other Countries of the Former Soviet Union, 1992–97, by Luis M. Valdivieso. 1998.

174. Impact of EMU on Selected Non–European Union Countries, by R. Feldman, K. Nashashibi, R. Nord, P. Allum, D. Desruelle, K. Enders, R. Kahn, and H. Temprano-Arroyo. 1998.

173. The Baltic Countries: From Economic Stabilization to EU Accession, by Julian Berengaut, Augusto Lopez-Claros, Françoise Le Gall, Dennis Jones, Richard Stern, Ann-Margret Westin, Effie Psalida, Pietro Garibaldi. 1998.

172. Capital Account Liberalization: Theoretical and Practical Aspects, by a staff team led by Barry Eichengreen and Michael Mussa, with Giovanni Dell'Ariccia, Enrica Detragiache, Gian Maria Milesi-Ferretti, and Andrew Tweedie. 1998.

171. Monetary Policy in Dollarized Economies, by Tomás Baliño, Adam Bennett, and Eduardo Borensztein. 1998.

170. The West African Economic and Monetary Union: Recent Developments and Policy Issues, by a staff team led by Ernesto Hernández-Catá and comprising Christian A. François, Paul Masson, Pascal Bouvier, Patrick Peroz, Dominique Desruelle, and Athanasios Vamvakidis. 1998.

169. Financial Sector Development in Sub-Saharan African Countries, by Hassanali Mehran, Piero Ugolini, Jean Phillipe Briffaux, George Iden, Tonny Lybek, Stephen Swaray, and Peter Hayward. 1998.

168. Exit Strategies: Policy Options for Countries Seeking Greater Exchange Rate Flexibility, by a staff team led by Barry Eichengreen and Paul Masson with Hugh Bredenkamp, Barry Johnston, Javier Hamann, Esteban Jadresic, and Inci Ötker. 1998.

167. Exchange Rate Assessment: Extensions of the Macroeconomic Balance Approach, edited by Peter Isard and Hamid Faruqee. 1998

166. Hedge Funds and Financial Market Dynamics, by a staff team led by Barry Eichengreen and Donald Mathieson with Bankim Chadha, Anne Jansen, Laura Kodres, and Sunil Sharma. 1998.

165. Algeria: Stabilization and Transition to the Market, by Karim Nashashibi, Patricia Alonso-Gamo, Stefania Bazzoni, Alain Féler, Nicole Laframboise, and Sebastian Paris Horvitz. 1998.

164. MULTIMOD Mark III: The Core Dynamic and Steady-State Model, by Douglas Laxton, Peter Isard, Hamid Faruqee, Eswar Prasad, and Bart Turtelboom. 1998.

163. Egypt: Beyond Stabilization, Toward a Dynamic Market Economy, by a staff team led by Howard Handy. 1998.

162. Fiscal Policy Rules, by George Kopits and Steven Symansky. 1998.

161. The Nordic Banking Crises: Pitfalls in Financial Liberalization? by Burkhard Dress and Ceyla Pazarbaşıoğlu. 1998.

160. Fiscal Reform in Low-Income Countries: Experience Under IMF-Supported Programs, by a staff team led by George T. Abed and comprising Liam Ebrill, Sanjeev Gupta, Benedict Clements, Ronald McMorran, Anthony Pellechio, Jerald Schiff, and Marijn Verhoeven. 1998.

159. Hungary: Economic Policies for Sustainable Growth, Carlo Cottarelli, Thomas Krueger, Reza Moghadam, Perry Perone, Edgardo Ruggiero, and Rachel van Elkan. 1998.

158. Transparency in Government Operations, by George Kopits and Jon Craig. 1998.

157. Central Bank Reforms in the Baltics, Russia, and the Other Countries of the Former Soviet Union, by a staff team led by Malcolm Knight and comprising Susana Almuiña, John Dalton, Inci Otker, Ceyla Pazarbaşıoğlu, Arne B. Petersen, Peter Quirk, Nicholas M. Roberts, Gabriel Sensenbrenner, and Jan Willem van der Vossen. 1997.

156. The ESAF at Ten Years: Economic Adjustment and Reform in Low-Income Countries, by the staff of the International Monetary Fund. 1997.

155. Fiscal Policy Issues During the Transition in Russia, by Augusto Lopez-Claros and Sergei V. Alexashenko. 1998.

154. Credibility Without Rules? Monetary Frameworks in the Post–Bretton Woods Era, by Carlo Cottarelli and Curzio Giannini. 1997.

153. Pension Regimes and Saving, by G.A. Mackenzie, Philip Gerson, and Alfredo Cuevas. 1997.

152. Hong Kong, China: Growth, Structural Change, and Economic Stability During the Transition, by John Dodsworth and Dubravko Mihaljek. 1997.

151. Currency Board Arrangements: Issues and Experiences, by a staff team led by Tomás J.T. Baliño and Charles Enoch. 1997.

150. Kuwait: From Reconstruction to Accumulation for Future Generations, by Nigel Andrew Chalk, Mohamed A. El-Erian, Susan J. Fennell, Alexei P. Kireyev, and John F. Wilson. 1997.

149. The Composition of Fiscal Adjustment and Growth: Lessons from Fiscal Reforms in Eight Economies, by G.A. Mackenzie, David W.H. Orsmond, and Philip R. Gerson. 1997.

148. Nigeria: Experience with Structural Adjustment, by Gary Moser, Scott Rogers, and Reinold van Til, with Robin Kibuka and Inutu Lukonga. 1997.

147. Aging Populations and Public Pension Schemes, by Sheetal K. Chand and Albert Jaeger. 1996.

146. Thailand: The Road to Sustained Growth, by Kalpana Kochhar, Louis Dicks-Mireaux, Balazs Horvath, Mauro Mecagni, Erik Offerdal, and Jianping Zhou. 1996.

145. Exchange Rate Movements and Their Impact on Trade and Investment in the APEC Region, by Takatoshi Ito, Peter Isard, Steven Symansky, and Tamim Bayoumi. 1996.

144. National Bank of Poland: The Road to Indirect Instruments, by Piero Ugolini. 1996.

143. Adjustment for Growth: The African Experience, by Michael T. Hadjimichael, Michael Nowak, Robert Sharer, and Amor Tahari. 1996.

142. Quasi-Fiscal Operations of Public Financial Institutions, by G.A. Mackenzie and Peter Stella. 1996.

141. Monetary and Exchange System Reforms in China: An Experiment in Gradualism, by Hassanali Mehran, Marc Quintyn, Tom Nordman, and Bernard Laurens. 1996.

140. Government Reform in New Zealand, by Graham C. Scott. 1996.

139. Reinvigorating Growth in Developing Countries: Lessons from Adjustment Policies in Eight Economies, by David Goldsbrough, Sharmini Coorey, Louis Dicks-Mireaux, Balazs Horvath, Kalpana Kochhar, Mauro Mecagni, Erik Offerdal, and Jianping Zhou. 1996.

138. Aftermath of the CFA Franc Devaluation, by Jean A.P. Clément, with Johannes Mueller, Stéphane Cossé, and Jean Le Dem. 1996.

137. The Lao People's Democratic Republic: Systemic Transformation and Adjustment, edited by Ichiro Otani and Chi Do Pham. 1996.

136. Jordan: Strategy for Adjustment and Growth, edited by Edouard Maciejewski and Ahsan Mansur. 1996.

135. Vietnam: Transition to a Market Economy, by John R. Dodsworth, Erich Spitäller, Michael Braulke, Keon Hyok Lee, Kenneth Miranda, Christian Mulder, Hisanobu Shishido, and Krishna Srinivasan. 1996.

134. India: Economic Reform and Growth, by Ajai Chopra, Charles Collyns, Richard Hemming, and Karen Parker with Woosik Chu and Oliver Fratzscher. 1995.

133. Policy Experiences and Issues in the Baltics, Russia, and Other Countries of the Former Soviet Union, edited by Daniel A. Citrin and Ashok K. Lahiri. 1995.

132. Financial Fragilities in Latin America: The 1980s and 1990s, by Liliana Rojas-Suárez and Steven R. Weisbrod. 1995.

131. Capital Account Convertibility: Review of Experience and Implications for IMF Policies, by staff teams headed by Peter J. Quirk and Owen Evans. 1995.

130. Challenges to the Swedish Welfare State, by Desmond Lachman, Adam Bennett, John H. Green, Robert Hagemann, and Ramana Ramaswamy. 1995.

Note: For information on the title and availability of Occasional Papers not listed, please consult the IMF Publications Catalog or contact IMF Publication Services.